OFFICIAL STRATEGY GUIDE

BY DAN BIRLEW

GUIDE MASTERY

This section will help you interpret the guide basics and the walkthrough elements. Each separate element represents itself. That is to say, the Tip in this section is representative of the Tips you'll find throughout the walkthrough. Use this section to your advantage.

MISSION INTRODUCTION

Each mission begins with a short summary of what is required to complete it. Told in the spirit of the Guidepost for the Hunters, the description reveals the objectives. Most objectives are achieved by killing a certain enemy or reaching a certain location, so pay attention to the clues in the phrases.

I know...

Look for pictures with captions throughout the walkthrough. These screenshots show the locations of hidden power-ups and items.

TIPS

Learn how the pros manage to dive into a battle or situation and come out unscathed. In addition, these tidbits may contain hints on how to improve your characters or your gameplay.

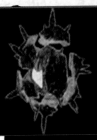

MONSTER TACTICS

The enemies frequently encountered in the game are mostly fodder for your hand cannons. However, these sections will expose the true weaknesses of your foes, so that you continue to have the advantage even in harder game modes. Look for them wherever new monsters are introduced into the game.

SECRET DOOR

SECRET ROOM

LEVEL 1

Certain doors that may appear to be useless at first glance sometimes lead to hidden locations from which the demons emanate. Defeat all the demons that appear in order to receive replenishing Green and White Orbs, and possibly even Blue Orb Fragments!

NOTES

At times, certain tidbits of information will need to be explained so that you get as much enjoyment out of the game as possible. Keep an eye out for these Note Boxes - they're sure to include some information that's worth your while.

BOSS FIGHTS

A few really tough individual monsters dominate all the legions of Hell. Dante must prove his heritage time and again to these boss monsters in order to free the world from the tyranny of the damned. These sections contain detailed strategies for defeating these master demons in all their forms.

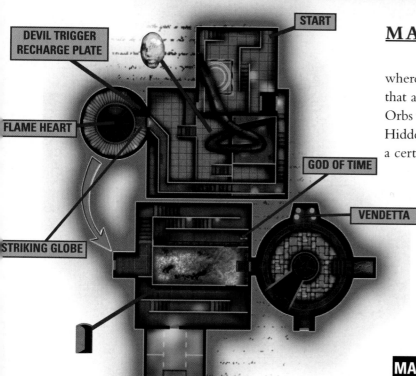

DEVIL TRIGGER
RECHARGE PLATE

START

FLAME HEART

GOD OF TIME

VENDETTA

STRIKING GLOBE

END LEVEL

MAPS

The maps provided in this guide show you where everything is. Here's a legend of the items that are regularly called out on the maps. The Red Orbs that litter the areas are not called out, but the Hidden Red Orbs that appear when you stand in a certain spot are clearly marked.

MAP LEGEND	
ITEM	**ICON**
RED ORB	
GOLD ORB	
GREEN ORB	
BLUE ORB	
BLUE ORB FRAGMENT	
SECRET DOOR	

DEMONIC POWER

Every devil hunter has to start off by learning the small stuff. Only the most complete combat training possible can aid the hunter in surmounting the chaotic hordes of Hell. This chapter summarizes the basic premises and systems of *Devil May Cry 2*. For more detailed information on the two main characters and their highly stylized fighting moves, read the Combat Mastery sections for Dante and Lucia.

ESSENTIAL CONTROLS

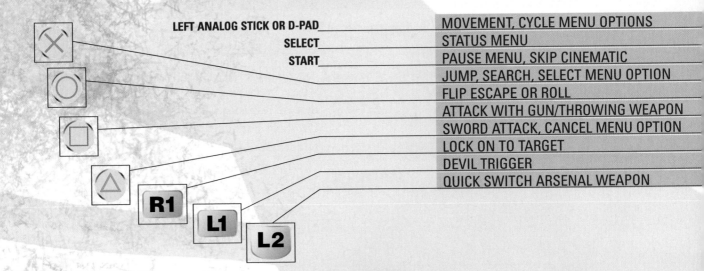

LEFT ANALOG STICK OR D-PAD	MOVEMENT, CYCLE MENU OPTIONS
SELECT	STATUS MENU
START	PAUSE MENU, SKIP CINEMATIC
	JUMP, SEARCH, SELECT MENU OPTION
	FLIP ESCAPE OR ROLL
	ATTACK WITH GUN/THROWING WEAPON
	SWORD ATTACK, CANCEL MENU OPTION
	LOCK ON TO TARGET
	DEVIL TRIGGER
	QUICK SWITCH ARSENAL WEAPON

MISSIONS

Before starting up either disc of *Devil May Cry 2*, consider your current skill level. Lucia completes fewer missions than Dante, and her chapters are considerably shorter and easier than are the veteran devil hunter's. Dante's missions are more difficult, sometimes involving awesome four-stage boss fights! If you haven't played the previous game in this series, you might consider tackling Lucia's disc first as a warm-up.

The two games contained in *Devil May Cry 2* are divided into short missions, each with a singular goal or objective. Sometimes the objective is to run through an area and find the exit. Other times, the sole point of the mission is to send a really powerful enemy straight back to Hell.

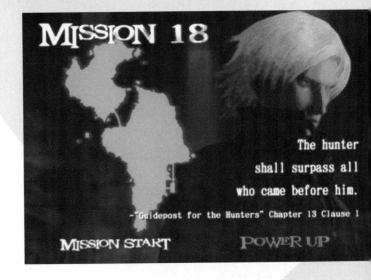

MISSION 18

The hunter shall surpass all who came before him.
-"Guidepost for the Hunters" Chapter 13 Clause 1

MISSION START   POWER UP

Every mission ends when the main goal is achieved. You'll be judged and graded based on the following criteria:

- The amount of time it took you to clear the mission
- The number of orbs collected from defeated foes
- The number of times you made the words "Show Time!!" appear onscreen
- The amount of damage inflicted on the character
- The number of items used during the mission

So the emphasis of the game is on playing very well and quickly, grabbing a whole lot of orbs and getting out without a scratch. The five grades you receive are averaged, and an overall Devil Hunter Rank is awarded. The highest rank for a mission is S (Superior). Only by obtaining an S rank on every mission will you unlock all the secrets of the game.

MOVEMENT

Although the game is set in a striking three-dimensional world, the control scheme works in a 2D fashion. This means that the controls are not tied to the characters' actual left or right, the controls are tied to the directions on the screen. So when you want the person to run toward the bottom of your television screen, press down on the Left Analog Stick. Press up when you want him or her to run back into the environment. If the person needs to run to the left side of the television monitor, then press that direction and they will head that way.

Camera angles usually change while the character crosses long areas of the game. However, just keep pressing the Left Analog Stick in the direction you already had it, and the character will keep moving forward from the previous camera angle into the next. For instance, let's say you are moving the character toward the camera by pressing down on the Left Analog Stick. Then the camera angle changes to a position behind the person. Just keep holding the Left Analog Stick in the position you've got it, and they will keep moving forward even if you're pressing in the opposite way. You do not have to move the stick to accommodate the new angle. When you stop, the functions of the Left Analog Stick will reset to reflect the directions contained in the new camera angle.

HUNTING

The path between the starting point and the finishing line isn't always a straight shot. The servants of the demon world have erected ancient puzzles and machinery to prevent the intrusion of unwanted guests. You must be skillful and savvy enough to figure out how to over come these obstacles and other roadblocks, sometimes in the form of giant devils that must die.

Clues are often given in short cinematic camera sweeps. Dante or Lucia will enter a room, and a brief survey of the area occurs. Often times, you are shown the entrance, the exit, and any other major features of the room that might factor into your ability to proceed. Don't be too hasty with that **START** button, or you'll cancel out your own clues!

To a large degree, the game is about jumping to places that most normal people couldn't reach. Therefore, if you're crossing an area and happen to spot a ledge high overhead, you should test your abilities and see if you can reach it. Sometimes landing on a high ledge releases a

dozen or more large Red Orbs hidden in an invisible pocket, just waiting for someone to stand in just the right spot. The game is full of these hidden caches and power ups, to test your resolve to explore the environment to the fullest.

Sometimes text messages are displayed when you search certain features of the environment, such as doors or pulsating membranes. By examining a door, wall panel or sewer grating, the player might find a Secret Room where extra enemies can be defeated and valuable orbs might be obtained—if you survive!

The mouth is open leaving a space

ENEMY APPEARANCES

While crossing areas, sets of demonic enemies materialize around the hunter and attack. The opponent group might be small at first. But as you eliminate members of the initial set, more foes will teleport into the area. The true size of an enemy set can only be judged when the last demon's skull is bouncing off the cobblestones.

Entering certain areas triggers enemy appearances. If you defeat the enemy group and remain in the general area where they appeared, the entire group will be triggered to reappear by your presence. Therefore, if you remain in one spot you'll keep having the same

battle over and over. This is one way to collect the orbs needed to upgrade those weapons, but it's also a time waster. A great mission ranking relies on a speedy achievement of the objectives. As a general rule of thumb, try to fight each enemy group once, and fight them well enough that the amount of orbs you receive is as large as possible.

DEVIL BOUNTY

The main reason to cut down devils in their tracks is for the orbs they release upon their demise. Like any modern bounty hunter, Dante and Lucia can redeem quantities of Red Orbs for useful items and upgrades. Improving the level and quality of your characters' weapons means that they will be able to do their jobs much more easily.

Most demons usually drop one or two medium-sized Red Orbs, plus a little Green Orb if you're low on vitality. However, the amount of Red Orbs divulged by a defeated foe can be multiplied greatly by striking a stylish combo.

STYLISH COMBO RATINGS

Certain powerful melee moves that each character is capable of performing have a strong chance of striking a stylish combo. When the game appreciates your combat prowess, some words appear on the right side of the screen. This is called "striking stylish", and the number of stylish combos you can achieve in a mission is counted as part of your overall grade. The immediate benefit of striking, maintaining and improving stylish combos is that while a high stylish rating is displayed onscreen, even low-level enemies will drop up to five times the amount of orbs than they would normally. A high stylish level also encourages enemies to drop helpful orbs such as White Orbs, Green Orbs and Holy Water, all of which are explained in the **Devilish Tools** chapter.

Once a stylish combo is struck, you must attack continuously to keep the words onscreen or they will slowly fade out. After the words disappear, the combo is ended and you'll have to start another from scratch. The easiest way to do this is to keep shooting enemies rapidly until you can get close enough to another foe and perform some more melee attacks. If you can attack with another move that is stylish, the words displayed will change and the color becomes redder. The color and phrasing of the words indicates the level at which your stylish combo stands:

Don't Worry
Come On!
Bingo!
Are You Ready?
Show Time!!

Certain moves of each character are more likely to strike a stylish combo, and these are indicated in the characters' chapters following this one. Actions that will keep a combo sustained so that the words remain onscreen include melee attacks, shooting enemies continuously, and rolling or Flip Escaping ○ during attacks. If your attacks miss an enemy or you take damage, the words will disappear from the screen instantly.

SHOPPING FOR DEMON SLAYERS

Proceeding through the first mission of either character, you'll encounter a statue depicting a lion-headed god holding an hourglass. This is a God of Time statue, a location where you can trade the Red Orbs you've collected from fallen foes for useful items as well as upgrades to your weapons. Before you start the second mission of either character, you can use the "Power Up" option on the Mission Start screen to purchase items and upgrades. Time spent perusing in the shop menu is counted against your mission ranking, so it's wiser to purchase things between missions when the clock is not ticking.

Using an item during a mission is heavily discouraged by the fact that you'll lose ranking points toward your mission grade. However, some circumstances call for emergency action, and it's always better to be prepared for those instances. The more you want to prepare, the more heavily you pay. The prices of goods and upgrades doubles each time you make a purchase, meaning it will take twice as long to raise your words and weapons to the next higher level.

EQUIPPING THE GOODS

Swords and arsenal weapons can be equipped by choosing the "Equip" option in the Status menu. The best weapons to use are the ones that enable you to cut down the enemies the fastest while sustaining the least damage yourself. For instance, Dante's sword Merciless is lightweight and swings in a slightly smoother arch with a faster frequency than his other melee weapons. However, it has all the stopping power

of a bee sting. While speed in combat is preferable against quick and evasive enemies, a light sword like Merciless is useless against giant goat headed demons that tend to walk right through sword slashes. Against more resilient demons with longer vitality bars, you'll want to equip a heavy weapon like the Vendetta

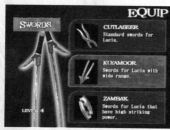

sword. Even though it swings more heavily than the Merciless, it has a better chance of knocking strong enemies on their backs.

The same holds true when equipping a firearm or throwing weapon. If you're plugging away with the Handguns or Throwing Darts and the enemies aren't even flinching, you might want to switch to something like the Shotgun or Darts. Although these weapons have slower rates of fire, they have greater stopping power and greater crowd-control capabilities. As you progress through the game, the number of enemies appearing onscreen at one time grows to a staggering amount. While the Handguns and Throwing Daggers are no doubt the most suave weapons each character uses, you really can't limit yourself to just these. For instance, if you're going to spend a half-hour fighting a possessed helicopter, you'll get a little tired of furiously tapping □. Give your thumb a rest by equipping a weapon like the Shotgun, which does twice the damage with half the shots.

Swords can only be equipped through the Equip screen, but the character's arsenal can be cycled by pressing L2. This is a handy function, but in the heat of battle you don't want to leave the character vulnerable while you cycle past the Submachine Guns and Shotgun to reach the Missile Launcher. During combat always equip weapons manually through the menus so that the action is paused and the character is always ready.

LOCK ON OR OFF?

Dante and Lucia automatically target the closest enemy, as indicated by a circular crosshair that marks the monster. By holding **R1**, this enemy will remain targeted even if other foes come within a closer range to the character. Also, most of the characters' special moves require you to hold the **R1** button to begin the attack.

Unlike most "survival horror" games by Capcom Entertainment, the lock on feature of *Devil May Cry 2* serves a very different function. In games like *Resident Evil* or *Dino Crisis*, the **R1** button must be held if you wish to fire a weapon at any point. But since Dante and Lucia automatically target enemies, holding **R1** is not required. In fact, the character will fight much better if you press **R1** only in the instances when it is absolutely needed.

The strategy of almost every enemy set is to surround or corner the devil hunters, and ambush them from all sides. If you use the lock on in every situation, you will be limiting the true fighting capabilities of the character. The enemy that is closest to the character is the most dangerous. It's best to leave your finger off **R1**, so that the character is always attacking the nearest foe. This is the surest way to clear the area around the character, and maintain a safe range from which to attack the enemies without receiving damage. Even if you've worn a foe down to a low vitality, it's always better to attack a more proximate threat in order to protect the character.

Lock on causes the character to focus on only one enemy. You'll want to lock on only in situations where the demon is almost defeated, and it tries to escape to regenerate its vitality. For instance, Savage Golems will attempt this every time you fight them. After you've chopped off the arms and upper torso of the creature, hold **R1** to lock onto the legs and continue saturating them with gunfire or thrown weapons. They will attempt to scamper off to the side of the area to regenerate their lost limbs and vitality. If allowed to escape, you'll have to fight the same enemy all over again from scratch!

Otherwise, the main use of lock on is to initiate special moves of the character that have a higher chance of striking a stylish combo. Once you've started the move, you can usually release your finger from the **R1** button and press the remaining buttons in the sequence to carry out these strong attacks.

SAVING DURING MISSIONS

One of the options on the Status menu is to save your progress. You can record your game data at any time to a PlayStation™ Memory Card. This is a good way to save the amount of orbs possessed and the number of Secret Rooms found. When you restart the game, you'll begin the mission from the starting point.

However, all of the Secret Rooms, Bonus Red Orbs, Gold Orbs, and Blue Orb Fragments you found on your last trip through will not reappear, since they've already been collected.

The benefit of saving before the completion of a mission is that you can play through once and waste time trying to make all those crazy jumps to reach bonus orbs and items. You can practice the special moves of the character, and spend all the time you want shopping at a God of Time statue. When you get close to the end of the mission, use the save function to record all that you've accomplished thus far. Then you can restart the mission, fly through the area without worrying about the secrets and hard to reach places, and accomplish the objectives in the short time required for an S ranking.

TRUE PAUSE

The clock is always ticking while the mission is underway, and each minute could be the difference between an excellent time ranking or a very sad clear time. If you must stop playing for a short time, the only way to pause your game is to press **START** and enter the Pause menu. Time does not continue to accrue in the mission while you are in this menu. However, if you enter the Status menu time keeps ticking. The moments you spend equipping weapons are counted as part of completing the mission, and so is any time used to browse in the shopping menu.

QUITTING OR RESTARTING MISSIONS

Pressing **SELECT** during the game brings up the Pause menu, and you'll notice that there are two reset options. "Quit the Mission" is the true reset option. Selecting to quit takes you back to the title screen. You must reload your last save to continue. None of the orbs or items you found during your first trip through the mission will be recorded, unless you saved the game before quitting.

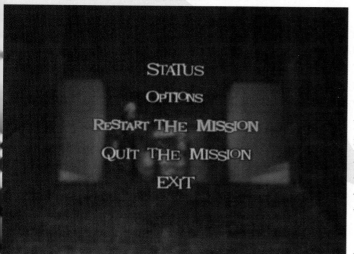

The option to "Restart the Mission" returns the game to the mission start screen. However, all of the orbs and items you found before restarting will still belong to you! Therefore, you could work your way through the mission, collect all the items and orbs, power up your weapons, find all the Secret Rooms, and then restart. On your second attempt at the mission, you can race through in a short amount of time and make a better ranking!

PRACTICE MAKES PERFECT

Although this guide aims to be the most complete resource for *Devil May Cry 2* available anywhere, the game is really a challenge of your skills and dedication as a gamer. While we take great pains to explain the moves and attacks of the characters, understanding and mastering these combinations is entirely up to you. We can't play the game for you; we can only show you how. In order to understand the abilities of each character and the attacks of each boss monster, you're going to have to see them for yourself. You are more likely to understand the topics that are discussed in this guidebook if you attempt to play the game for a while by yourself. The main intention of this guide is to help you master the concepts of game, to better understand the weaknesses of the enemies, and to find things you might have missed on your first trial.

With that said, the next two chapters contain pages of moves and tricks for you to practice until you get them right. Only by mastering all the abilities that the protagonists offer can you actually play the game in a style befitting a true devil hunter!

DEVILISH TOOLS

ITEMS

When vitality is running low and the devils are closing in for the kill, you can use items to regain your strength and send the hell spawn back whence they came.

OBTAINING ITEMS

Each character starts off with a Vital Star S. and a Devil Star S. Most items are purchased from God of Time statues, or through the Power Up option before each mission starts. To purchase items, you must collect Red Orbs released by enemies that are defeated or from the environment.

Usually, each item you purchase causes the price to rise. For instance, the first Vital Star S. purchased costs 1000 Red Orbs. If you want to buy another, it will cost 2000 Red Orbs. The cost continues to multiply until you have purchased five of the item, and the market levels off for the remainder of your purchases. This rise in cost is to dissuade you from relying on the use of items, since they lower your mission ranking.

USING ITEMS

To use an item during combat, press SELECT to enter the Status menu. Choose the Item option, and use the Left Analog Stick to select an item to use.

At the end of each mission, you'll receive a Devil Hunter Rank that summarizes your efforts. Using items lowers the "Item Used" grade by roughly one letter per item consumed, and detracts from your overall Devil Hunter Rank.

RED ORB

A crystal with condensed demon blood, used to gain new power. One or more Red Orbs are released when each enemy is destroyed. To collect Red Orbs, move your character toward them and the characters' devil essence will attract these little red balls. To view the number of Red Orbs in possession, enter the Power Up menu or the Item menu. Also, pressing **R1** during the game will display the quantity held in the upper right corner. Red Orbs can be traded at a God of Time statue or the Power Up menu for items and upgrades to weapons.

GOLD ORB

A crystal generated by the immortals, containing the power of resurrection. Only one Gold Orb can be possessed at a time. When the character with a Gold Orb is killed, he or she will automatically come back to life with full vitality and Devil Trigger gauges. Gold Orbs are valuable, and are often hidden. Sometimes they are even used as bait by the demons, to ambush the characters. When a Gold Orb is found during a mission, 100 Red Orbs are also added to the quantity held by the player. Gold Orbs can be purchased from a God of Time statue or through the Power Up screen before a mission. The cost to purchase Gold Orbs will double for the first three purchases.

GOLD ORB COSTS	
1ST	10000
2ND	20000
3RD+	40000 (MAX PRICE)*

*All Gold Orbs purchased after the 3rd cost 20000 Red Orbs.

WHITE ORB

A crystal with condensed demon tears that will restore energy to the Devil Trigger Gauges. Enemies sometimes drop White Orbs when the character is low on Devil Trigger power. If you manage to kill the entire monster set with a high stylish combo and don't take a scratch, the chances are even higher. White Orbs are always obtained by clearing Secret Rooms.

BLUE ORB

A crystal with vital force that increases the capacity of the vitality meter. After a number of Blue Orbs have been found or assembled, the vitality meter of the character becomes longer. When the meter reaches the maximum graphic length, it will double over and fill twice. Blue Orbs are hidden in hard to reach spots in various missions. Finding four Blue Orb Fragments can also produce them. Five Blue Orbs can be purchased from the God of Time statues or through the Power Up screen before a mission.

BLUE ORB COSTS	
1ST	3000
2ND	6000
3RD	10000
4TH	15000
5TH (MAX)	20000

GREEN ORB

A crystal with condensed demon fluid, which will restore vitality for those who bear demon blood. Defeated enemies sometimes drop Green Orbs when the character's vitality meter is low, when the player has fought with excellence and a high stylish combo rating. They can also be obtained by smashing certain objects in the environment, and by conquering the enemies encountered in Secret Rooms.

VITAL STAR L.

A special stone imbued with a demon's vital force that recovers a large amount of vitality. A Vital Star L. must be used from the Item menu, and it will restore approximately one full line of vitality in the character's gauge. As finding and assembling Blue Orbs extends the vitality meter, use of one or more Vital Star L. is the only certain method of recovering large amounts of vitality. They must be purchased from a God of Time statue or through the Power Up screen before missions, at a rising cost per purchase until the third item is bought. The character can hold ten of these at a time.

VITAL STAR L. COSTS	
1ST	2000
2ND	4000
3RD+	8000 (MAX PRICE)*

*All Vital Star L. purchased after the 3rd cost 8000 Red Orbs.

BLUE ORB FRAGMENT

A fragment of a vital energy orb. When four of these are found, they will be automatically assembled into one Blue Orb, and the vitality meter will increase in length. The number of Blue Orb Fragments possessed by the character can be viewed in the Item menu. Blue Orb Fragments are obtained by searching hidden and hard to reach areas, and also by finding and conquering certain Secret Rooms.

PURPLE ORB

A crystal containing the soul of an arch devil, which will increase the length of the Devil Trigger gauge. The only way to obtain Purple Orbs is by purchasing them through the God of Time statue shops or the Power Up screen before each mission. When the Devil Trigger meter is increased, the character can remain transformed for longer periods and cause more damage with attacks.

PURPLE ORB COSTS	
1ST	3000
2ND	6000
3RD	10000
4TH	15000
5TH (MAX)	20000

VITAL STAR S.

A special stone with vital force that recovers a small amount of vitality. Each character begins the game with one of these in their inventory. Use of a Vital Star S. will restore approximately half of a full line of vitality. Therefore, as the characters' vitality meters are extended to the point of doubling over, these items will become less useful in recovering health. Vital Star S. can only be purchased from a God of Time statue or through the Power Up screen before a mission, and the cost will rise per purchase for the first five transactions. The character can hold 30 of these at a time.

VITAL STAR S. COSTS	
1ST	1000
2ND	2000
3RD	3000
4TH	4000
5TH+	5000 (MAX PRICE)*

*All Vital Star S. purchased after the 5th cost 5000 Red Orbs.

DEVIL STAR L.

A special stone imbued with a demon's energy that restores a large amount of power in the Devil Trigger meter. A Devil Star L. must be used from the Item menu, and it will restore approximately one full line of power in the character's gauge. They must be purchased from a God of Time statue or through the Power Up screen before missions, at a rising cost per purchase until the third item is bought.

DEVIL STAR L. COSTS	
1ST	3000
2ND	6000
3RD+	12000 (MAX PRICE)*

*All Devil Star L. purchased after the 3rd cost 12000 Red Orbs.

DEVIL STAR S.

A special stone that restores a small amount of power in the Devil Trigger meter. Each character begins the game with one of these in their inventory. Use of a Devil Star S. will restore approximately half of a fully extended Devil Trigger meter. Devil Star S. can only be purchased from a God of Time statue or through the Power Up screen before a mission, and the cost will rise per purchase for the first five transactions.

DEVIL STAR S. COSTS	
1ST	1000
2ND	3000
3RD	5000
4TH	7000
5TH+	10000 (MAX PRICE)*

*All Devil Star S. purchased after the 5th cost 10000 Red Orbs.

HOLY STAR

A special stone of divine blessing that purifies the body. Several enemies use attacks that will poison the character for a full minute. Poisoning is denoted by a purplish glow surrounding the character, and the vitality meter flashes purple as well. Vitality will slowly diminish while poisoning is in effect. Use of a Holy Star will negate poison instantly. Each character can carry up to 99 of these. The only way to obtain a Holy Star is by purchasing them through the God of Time statues or through the Power Up screen before a mission. Each Holy Star costs 1000 Red Orbs, without an increase in price.

HOLY WATER

A special powder blue colored orb released by defeated demons sometimes during battle. When Dante collects these special orbs along with the others, all enemies are instantly killed. Boss monsters will take heavy damage, if they are in the vicinity as well. Holy Waters are more likely to be released by defeated enemies when the stylish combo level is high, and when the character has not taken any damage during the current battle.

SMELL OF FEAR

Condensed emotion of the demons, which can be used to negate damage from the next three attacks by any enemy. When this item is used from the Item menu, the character pulsates with white light. The effect continues until the character receives three hits from any type of enemy. The effect of negation prevents any vitality from being subtracted from the meter, and the character cannot be stunned or knocked down by strong enemy attacks. The only way to obtain a Smell of Fear vial is through the God of Time statues or through the Power Up screen before a mission. The character can hold three at a time, and the cost doubles for the first three purchases.

SMELL OF FEAR COSTS	
1ST	5000
2ND	10000
3RD+	20000 (MAX PRICE)*

*All Smell of Fear purchased after the 3rd cost 20000 Red Orbs.

AMULET STONES

The demon blood coursing through the veins of the heroes enables them to transform into powerful creatures of destruction. But their human side limits this transformation to a short period of time. The half-human, half-demon hunters are capable of modifying the powers of their transformed state, called Devil Trigger, by wearing certain magic amulets.

Amulet Stones inserted into these amulets enhance their abilities while in Devil Trigger. Crescent moon-shaped stones add new abilities such as improved swimming or running, or even flying. Circular stones add the power of magical elements to attacks, so that fire, ice or lightning occurs while fighting. Teardrop stones allow the wearer to regain health, deal double damage, or even stop enemies in their tracks. Three of these stones can be inserted into the amulet at one time, one of each shape.

AQUA HEART

For Lucia's use only during her underwater missions, this magic stone enables faster swimming and maneuvering while underwater in Devil Trigger mode. She moves through the water at much faster speed, and also rises or descends faster.

AERIAL HEART

Lucia and Dante both gain the power to fly in Devil Trigger when this stone is equipped in their amulets. Press ✕ to jump off the ground and spread the character's wings. Move the Left Analog Stick to fly around. Tap ✕ rapidly to ascend straight up. To rise slowly while flying, hold ✕. To descend more quickly than normal, hold ○. Certain attacks such as Air Raid and Round Trip can only be performed while flying in the air. When the ground is a dangerous place, use this to fly above enemies and attack from the air. Sometimes, the only way to continue is by flying to an exit near the ceiling of a room.

QUICK HEART

Either character can greatly increase ground-running and attack speeds while in Devil Trigger by equipping this stone in the amulet. When the character needs to cross long areas or run behind an enemy very quickly, this heart is sure to help succeed.

FLAME HEART

When this stone is equipped in the characters' round slot on the amulet, all of their attacks while in Devil Trigger will unleash the power of fire. Bullets that strike the skin of enemies will explode into flame. The blades of the heroes shall burn as they slice through flesh and bone. Most demons are weak against the hell fire, but those that use fire attacks will be strong against it. Creatures that use ice attacks or live underwater will be weak against the power of fire, and will succumb more easily when this stone is equipped.

FROST HEART

The characters' Devil Trigger attacks will chill demons to the core when this stone is equipped in the amulet. Demons that specialize in fire attacks should be particularly weak against attacks enhanced with this effect. Devils who are slightly blue in appearance or dwell in the water will suffer little damage from frost.

ELECTRO HEART

The power of lightning has a strong effect upon demons that rely on metal armor and weapons. When this stone is equipped in the amulet, their weakness can be exploited while the character is in Devil Trigger. Unfortunately, few demons fit that bill.

EVIL HEART

Appearing only during Lucia's missions, the Evil Heart is a cursed object that drains the vitality of a devil hunter while it is possessed. Lucia is inflicted with this item for a short time, and must insert it into a slot within the Power Plant in order to be rid of it. The Evil Heart will be converted into the Electro Heart for her. While the Evil Heart is draining Lucia's life, equip the Healing Heart and Devil Trigger occasionally to regain vitality lost to the effects of the curse

HEALING HEART

With the Healing Heart equipped in the amulet, the possessor gains the ability to regenerate vitality while in Devil Trigger. The restorative effect fights the debilitation of negative ailments such as poisoning, and vitality draining items such as the Evil Heart. Whenever you are fighting long boss battles or navigating through areas where few Green Orbs are found, equip the Healing Heart to remain health during each Devil Trigger.

OFFENCE HEART

Although the characters inflict an intense amount of damage to enemies while they remain in Devil Trigger, that effect can be nearly doubled by equipping the Offence Heart in the amulet. The damage of the characters' arsenal receives the most apparent boost, allowing Dante and Lucia to do more damage than ever with gunfire and thrown weapons.

CHRONO HEART

When this stone is inserted into the teardrop shaped indention in the amulet, the possessor gains the ability to move at a speed much faster than the demons. Each time a person equipped with this enters Devil Trigger, the enemies onscreen will move in short jerks only. The user has time to strike each enemy several times before they move a single step.

AMULET STONES

PATH 1: THE HUNTER

The path of the Hunter is lined on all sides by the machinations of the wicked and the despised. Great are the chal-lenges that arise, but great also are the skills and the knowledge of the Hunter. Utilizing those skills and experience to surmoun each obstacle requires a compendium of foreknowledge and expertise the likes of which are found herein.

COMBAT MASTERY

Long ago, the devils ruling the Underworld combined forces in an attempt to invade and overthrow the world of the humans A lone demon knight took pity upon mortals, and with his newfound sense of justice set out to defeat the demons and send them back whenc they came. The name of this legendary knight was Sparda, and his story became renown in the Gnostic annals of supernatural history.

Several millennia passed, and a new threat rose against the mortal world from the demon kind. The ancient devil Mundus, lead-ing an army of demonic creations, dispatched his four most trusted lieutenants to prepare for him a gateway into the world of the human on Mallet Island. His plans to dominate the mortal dimension might have come to fruition, but he did not count on one element to come into play: Sparda begot a son by a mortal woman, the half-human half-demon Dante.

Having lost his mother and brother during an attack by demons several years prior, Dante established a private investigation firn specializing in hunting down and destroying supernatural creatures wherever they appear. The extermination services of the Devil May Cry detective agency can be purchased merely by uttering "the password", which can only be obtained through certain underground connec-tions.

With the combined strength of his father's heritage and the weapons of the devils that were passed down to him, Dante reclaimed the powers buried within him and followed in his father's footsteps. Dante defeated Mundus and his devils, and sealed the breach between the mortal realm and the underworld.

Several years have passed. Dante is summoned by the Protectorate, a race of half-human, half-demon devil hunters such as him-self, who have protected the ancient islands of Vidu Mali from the return of the devils that used to control the area. Flipping his trademark coin of Fate, Dante takes the assignment and sets off for Vidu Mali. His heritage is called upon once more to seal a rift between the worlds forced by the demons that wish to enslave mankind.

BASIC SKILLS

Dante dispatches the creatures of the demon world with extreme prejudice, utilizing a sword and firearms. All of the move detailed in this section are valid ways to continue a stylish combo once it has been sparked.

Shooting

Dante brings with him a pair of well-oiled, rapid-fire automatic Handguns into the fray. Press □ to shoot at targeted enemies. Tap □ rapidly to fire at a higher rate.

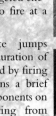

When Dante jumps high into the sky, the duration of his leap can be suspended by firing from midair. Dante gains a brief aerial advantage over opponents on the ground by shooting from above. While in the air, tap the □ button rapidly to fire during the descent. Weapons with a lower firing rate, such as the Shotgun, will fire only two or three times during a single jump.

Sword Combo

Press △ to use Dante's sword. In addition to defeating enemies, the sword is useful for destroying breakable objects in the environment, such as statues and furniture. Sometimes hidden orbs are released through such action. Certain key objects, such as blue globes, must be struck repeatedly with the sword until they activate and open new areas of the environment.

Press △ in succession and Dante will perform a series of three diagonal slashes, followed by a spinning slash finish. This combination of sword strokes can be modified into more powerful versions when the Left Analog Stick is moved in a certain direction with the correct timing. Such moves might spark a stylish combo, and so they are listed in the following section.

Rolling

Press ○ to make Dante roll forward. Rolling is useful for moving Dante to another position quickly, such as avoiding enemy attacks. You might also try rolling if you want to dive for a Red Orb that's about to expire and disappear. Used in combination with shooting, rolling can be used to maintain a stylish combo while you get closer to an enemy. The direction of the roll is determined by pressing the left stick in a certain direction

Jumping

Press ✗ to jump in the air. The direction of the jump can be modified while in midair by pressing the Left Analog Stick after ✗ is pressed. Use this midair control function to hop onto low platforms and ledges.

By pressing the Left Analog Stick in any direction at the moment ✗ is pressed, you can make Dante flip in midair. This move will carry him farther through the air in the given direction.

Flip Escape

While fighting an enemy, hold [R1] to lock on. Move the Left Analog Stick away from the enemy or to the left or right, and press ○. Dante will flip in the given direction. There is a certain amount of invulnerability that occurs while Dante is in motion, so this move can be used to dodge right past projectiles and attacks. If a Flip Escape is executed successfully during the instant an attack misses, it could spark or improve a stylish combo.

Air Hike

After jumping, press ✗ while Dante is in midair to double-jump. When the Air Hike is performed without use of the Left Analog Stick, Dante leaps straight up and then performs a back flip. If you press the Left Analog Stick in any direction during the first or second jump of the air hike, Dante

will flip in that direction. For careful jumps onto higher platforms and ledges, jump straight up and press the Left Analog Stick during the second jump to control Dante's direction.

Kick Jump

While moving toward or facing a wall, press ✗ to jump and then press it again while holding the Left Analog Stick toward the wall. At the height of the first leap, Dante makes contact with the wall and then springs upward like a cat to gain extra height. This is the move to use for leaping up a series of ledges.

Wall Hike

While facing a wall, press ○ to start a wall hike. Dante runs up the wall, then backflips away from the surface and lands a few yards away. This is a very effective method to avoid getting cornered by enemies.

A Wall Hike allows Dante to reach a higher level than an initial jump off the ground, such as at the start of a Kick Jump. Also, when Dante backflips off the wall, press ✗ while he's in midair to add a second jump to the move. Moving the Left Analog Stick simultaneously can control the direction of the second jump.

Wall Run

In a slight variation, press ○ while running alongside a wall to perform a Wall Run. Dante continues moving forward while running up onto the vertical surface. After a few steps, he will leap off the wall, then flip in midair to carry himself forward and land.

A second jump can also be added to this move by pressing ✗ after Dante leaps off the wall. Move the Left Analog Stick at the moment ✗ is pressed to control the direction of the second jump.

SHOULDER BUTT

Hold the [R1] button while jumping. The instant Dante lands on the ground, press △ with exact timing. Dante steps toward the closest enemy and butts them with his shoulder, just hard enough to knock over most foes. While this can be a tricky move to learn, it helps to clear the landing area for any jump.

SPECIAL MOVES

In addition to the basic moves that Dante performs rather easily, he also has a cache of special combat attacks and actions that enable him to generate and improve stylish combos. All of the moves listed in this section have the ability to start a stylish combo, or to raise an already existing combo to the next level.

High Time (Short)

While facing an enemy, hold R1 and move the Left Analog Stick in the direction *away* from the foe. Press ⚠ simultaneously and Dante will bash the demon up into the air. At this point, you can leap into the air beside the foe and bash them back down to the ground, or you can whip out some firearms and try to juggle them in midair. This is the shorter version of High Time.

High Time (Complete)

The complete version of High Time is initiated by holding R1 while moving the Left Analog Stick in the direction away from the enemy, then pressing ⚠ *hard* so that when Dante bashes the opponent, he flies into the air beside them. Continue holding R1, and with the proper timing press ⚠ to make Dante kick the opponent in midair. Continue your lucky streak by pressing ⚠ with the right timing again, and Dante will backflip to kick the helpless foe once more. Finally, press ⚠ one more time, and Dante will smash the enemy to the ground with his sword. All of this occurs almost instantly while in midair! It's a tricky move to execute, and most low-level enemies in Normal Mode won't last through the first two blows, but the thrill of executing this move perfectly is overwhelming, so start practicing!

Stinger

While facing the enemy, hold R1 and move the Left Analog Stick in the direction *toward* the opponent, then press ⚠. Dante slides a medium distance across the ground, and spears the opponent with an extremely hard stab. This move is excellent to use against foes in a cluster—it will knock the whole group to the ground.

Spin Bash

Hold the Left Analog Stick in a direction *away* from the target while pressing ⚠ to initiate a sword attack. As you continue pressing ⚠, Dante will perform two quick lateral slashes, followed by a hard spinning slash. The speed of this attack, as well as the short balance recovery time, allows Dante to initiate the next attack quicker. This is a very effective move for elevating stylish combos already in effect, and a great way to attack Striking Stones for all the orbs they're worth!

Extended Sword Combo

Start a normal Sword Combo, and then extend the series of attacks by moving the Left Analog Stick in the direction *away* from the target. Dante will add four more slashes to the combo, finishing in a powerful crouching slash. This is a great move to use against opponents with long vitality bars who need lots of punishment in one go. The final move effectively knocks even large opponents far away.

Chop Combo

Start a normal Sword Combo, and then move the Left Analog Stick *toward* the direction of the target after the second stroke. Begin tapping ⚠ rapidly. After the third stroke, Dante suddenly hops upward and chops the opponent in half, then brings his sword straight back up through them! Even very tall enemies will be flung into the air by this amusing combo.

Twosome Time

While shooting at a target, enemies may attempt to ambush Dante from the side or behind. As the second enemy approaches, increase your rate of fire on the targeted enemy by tapping ◻ rapidly, then move the Left Analog Stick toward the enemy that is close behind or to the side of Dante. He will point one of his guns at the foe and blast them away.

This move may be easier to execute if you first lock on to the prime target by holding the R1 button, then move the Left Analog Stick toward the oncoming foe. Dante steps sideways to shoot at enemies in front and behind, crosses arms to shoot at an opponent to the side, or possibly even reaches behind his head to ward off an oncoming ambush. There is a slight chance while performing any of these defensive moves that Dante will strike or improve the level of a stylish combo.

Rain Storm

Air Hike high into the air directly above enemies. At the apex of the jump, Dante flips over. As his head is pointed toward the ground, press ◻ rapidly and Dante will shoot at the enemies below as he dives headfirst out of the sky. With kamikaze flare, Dante is capable of knocking many types of foes right off their feet with this move, and may strike stylish in the bargain.

DEVIL TRIGGER

Dante is capable of releasing the evil powers in his blood, transforming into a crimson winged demon capable of utter devastation, known in certain circles as "Devil Man". The term "Devil Trigger" refers to this state of transformation, as well as the power that is contained in the meter. All of Dante's attacks gain a tremendous amount of power while he is transformed. Dante gains the ability to perform certain special attacks that are only available while Devil Trigger lasts. However, because of his half-human lineage, this transformation can be maintained for only a short duration. Once the power contained in his Devil Trigger gauges runs out, Dante reverts to his normal form and level of strength.

By equipping magical stones in his amulet, Dante gains certain powers and abilities while "in" Devil Trigger. These stones enable him to focus his powers to use the magical elements of fire, ice, and electricity against opponents with his attacks. He can also gain the ability to fly through the air, or to run across the ground at ten times his normal speed. Devil Trigger can also be used to regain vitality and stop time. All the details are covered in the **Amulet Stones** chapter of this guide.

Dante starts each mission with a full vitality bar and empty Devil Trigger gauges. Pain is the imminent principle of Hell, and so for every point of damage Dante inflicts or sustains, his Devil Trigger gauges are filled just a little bit. Melee attacks with swords will fill the Devil Trigger gauges more quickly than attacks with firearms. Devil Trigger power can also be gained by using a Devil Star item, or by purchasing a Purple Orb to extend the length of the meter before a mission. As the Devil Trigger gauge is elongated, Dante becomes able to remain in this hyperactive state for longer periods of time.

When the Devil Trigger gauges are gray, Dante cannot transform. Once the gauge turns a certain color, representing the elemental stone of power equipped in the amulet, press L1 to enter Devil Trigger. Dante can usually transform when the Devil Trigger meter fills up to the first gauge line.

Running

While in Devil Trigger, Dante runs at a speed much faster than normal. Crossing long distances requires less time when Devil Trigger can be used to move. When the Quick Heart is obtained during the game and equipped in the amulet, even the faster movement speed of Devil Trigger is further increased! With the Quick Heart, Dante can cross incredibly long distances in a matter of seconds, rather than a whole minute. Speed is also integral in escaping from enemies or running behind them before they can target or follow Dante.

Flip Chop

While Dante is in Devil Trigger and fighting an opponent, press ▲ repeatedly to begin a Sword Combo. After the first swing, move the Left Analog Stick toward or away from the direction Dante is facing and continue pressing ▲. Dante's second attack is a quick thrust at the target. He then flips over and chops them down the middle with his sword.

Multi-sword

While Dante is in Devil Trigger and fighting an opponent, press ▲ repeatedly to begin a Sword Combo. After the second swing, move the Left Analog Stick toward or away from the direction Dante faces and tap ▲ rapidly. Dante pulls his arm back to charge up the third attack, then unleashes a series of rapid-fire thrusts that move so fast, only the faintest outline of the sword can be seen.

Pole Kick

While Dante is in Devil Trigger and fighting an opponent, press ▲ repeatedly to begin a Sword Combo. After the third swing of the usual four-swing combo, move the Left Analog Stick toward or away from the direction Dante faces and tap ▲ rapidly. Devil Man stabs his sword into the pavement, then uses it as a pole to swing around and deliver a powerful kick to an opponent.

Flying

Devil Man gains the ability to hover and soar through the air when the Aerial Heart is obtained during the course of the game. Air Hike into the air and Devil Trigger midair while the Aerial Heart is equipped. Dante spreads his wings, and begins to slowly descend if you do not act. Move the Left Analog Stick to fly across the area. Press ✕ to ascend straight upward, and tap ✕ repeatedly to continue rising. Hold ✕ while moving the Left Analog Stick, and Dante will maintain a certain altitude above the ground. To descend at a slightly faster rate than the usual, hold ○ while hovering or flying.

There are limitations to flying, as Dante will rise to only a certain height above the surface. In some areas, this limitation is disabled for a special reason, and you can fly up several levels to the top of a large chamber if you desire. However, flying in Devil Trigger is prohibited in areas where a good deal of platform jumping is required.

Certain attacks become available only when Dante is in Devil Trigger *and* flying off the ground.

Air Raid

While flying in Devil Trigger, press and hold □ to release a rapid fire series of blasts from above. Lay your thumb over the □ and ✕ buttons simultaneously, so that Dante maintains altitude while shooting.

Round Trip

While flying in Devil Trigger, press ▲ to launch Dante's sword spinning in an arch around the transformed devil hunter. The attack delivers massive damage to all flying or tall opponents in range. This attack can also be used to quickly activate key globe objects that are floating in the air during Dante's Mission 14.

Impaling

While flying in Devil Trigger, hold R1 while pressing the Left Analog Stick down, then press ▲. Dante shoots downward to the surface and stabs through anything directly beneath him. This powerful attack can also be executed after performing an Air Raid while in Devil Trigger.

WEAPONS

SWORDS

Melee attacks are the key to striking stylish combos and dealing the most damage. Additionally, attacking enemies with swords fills the Devil Trigger gauges of either hero much faster than gunfire. However, this style of combat requires the most precision, and a firm knowledge of the weapons available to the devil hunters.

Improving Swords

All swords start off at level 1, and upgrades can be purchased at any God of Time statue or in the Power Up screen before a mission. Swords have five levels. Although the first upgrade is relatively low in cost of Red

Orbs, improving a sword to its maximum level is a costly venture overall. The higher the level of the sword, the greater its attack power is and the sooner it will strike a stylish combo. Since swords provide the start of all stylish combos, increasing their level takes precedence over improving the levels of firearms or throwing weapons.

SWORD ENHANCEMENTS

LEVEL	RED ORB COST
LV1	0
LV2	5000
LV3	10000
LV4	20000
LV5	40000

REBELLION

Rebellion is a well-balanced weapon that Dante brings to the hunt. It's a standard sword with medium range and a fair striking power. You will certainly desire more chopping power against taller foes, or those with thick shells or skins. However, throughout the game Rebellion remains the best weapon to use against Agonofinis, Terreofinis, Mortfinis, and all the various types of Msira.

MERCILESS

A long, thin blade found in the Temple of the Arcana, Merciless has a longer range than Dante's other swords, giving him a slight advantage over enemies who tend to be elusive. However, what it gains in length, it sacrifices in strength as Merciless has a slightly lower striking power. Still, this is the best weapon to use against enemies such as Pyromancers, Auromancers, and Brontomancers, as well airborne enemies like Puia and Sargassos.

VENDETTA

The Vendetta is a heavy blade found in the Power Plant. Its short range and heavy weight is compensated for by an overwhelming chopping power, making Vendetta the weapon of choice against tall or thick skinned enemies such as all types of goat demons, Demonochorus that have fallen to the ground, and Savage Golems. Dante swings this sword at a slightly slower rate than other weapons, so it's not a good idea to trade power for speed against the more agile enemies.

GUNS

Whereas swords and special moves are the starting point of any stylish combo, a good devil hunter needs the rapid fire power to carry it through. After striking a stylish combo and defeating any enemy, blast away with these firearms and thrown projectiles to keep those lovely colored words onscreen. The entire game can be won simply by shooting foes, but it's a long and hard road. Use all weapons in the arsenal in combination with melee swords to eliminate foes efficiently and stylishly.

Improving Guns and Projectiles

Side arms and thrown weapons all have only two levels. Improving the characters' secondary weapons takes a back seat to enhancing their swords, which are the tools used to strike stylish combos. Level 1 Handguns can sustain a stylish combo just as well as when they're at level 3. However, once you manage to improve an arsenal weapon, you'll find that your characters have greater stopping power against larger foes and flying enemies, in addition to inflicting more damage.

GUN ENHANCEMENTS

LEVEL	RED ORB COST
LV1	0
LV2	10000
LV3	30000

HANDGUNS

Custom-made by Dante himself, these twin automatics, known in certain circles as "Ebony and Ivory", are specially designed to allow the devil hunter to focus his magic energy through the bullets and into his supernatural targets. Their lightweight and easy sliding bridges enable Dante a fair amount of freedom to move and dodge while firing. These are the ultimate weapons for the performance of Dante's cool new moves, such as Twosome Time and Rain Storm. Packing medium firepower with a high rate of fire, the Handguns are perfect for taking on most enemies in the game.

SUBMACHINE GUNS

This set of compact Submachine guns allows Dante to fire at a single target with a high rate of accuracy. However, these guns aren't as powerful as you might imagine since they spray low-caliber bullets at supernatural enemies. While the Submachine guns will help to hold large devils at bay, their constant vibrating recoil forces Dante to hold them in front at all times. He cannot perform defensive moves, like Twosome Time, and so he is somewhat more vulnerable from the sides and flank. Still, these are great weapons to use when your thumb is tired of rapping on the fire button so quickly!

SHOTGUN

With this sawed-off double barrel shotgun at his disposal, Dante can blast all enemies in a wide area directly in front of himself. The gun must be cocked after each firing, which Dante handles rather rapidly. Still, if you're fighting swift predators like Msira, then there is a split second of vulnerability during the reloading motion that you might want to avoid. The shotgun has awesome stopping power, blowing even large goat-headed demons away from Dante with frightening force. This is a great weapon for spreading out a group of enemies attempting to surround Dante. While using the Shotgun, Dante keeps one of his Handguns ready to blast away enemies approaching from the side or rear in Twosome Time style.

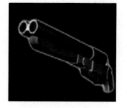

MISSILE LAUNCHER

This elongated surface-to-air missile launcher fires a missile in a straight line toward the target. The force of the blast causes massive damage through a direct hit. Plus, any foes in the direct vicinity of the blast will take heavy damage and possibly be thrown to the ground—quite a nasty site, indeed! However, the rate of fire on this weapon takes some getting used to. You'll certainly want to Flip Escape to the left or right after each shot, because enemies on the sidelines will certainly fire projectile attacks while you are shooting. Plus, Dante can fire the weapon only while his feet are firmly planted on the ground. When using the Missile Launcher, Dante keeps one of his Handguns ready to blow away enemies approaching from the rear or the flank. Also, if you attempt to fire while jumping, Dante uses the single Handgun in the air.

MISSION 1

"Toward the north, the hunter of dark blood will realize his destiny. The protector of the land has marked the rendezvous point on the map. The hunter must navigate through the lands where the darklings have infested, where the living fear to tread in the streets. Upon suppression of an insurmountable number of foes, the key to a gateway is bestowed. The hunter shall then arrive at the outpost of the summoner."

–Guidepost for the Hunters *Chapter 1 Clause 3*

TOWER BASE

In the large area below the clock tower, take a few moments to get acquainted with Dante's movements, attacks and actions. You won't be able to practice all Dante's attacks until he is actually facing an enemy, but at least you'll be ready to roll into battle blazing. Smash the two gargoyle statues for **Red Orbs**, which can be exchanged for useful items and weapon power-ups.

Don't miss the large Red Orb near the ugly face on the north side.

Smash the gargoyle statue on the south side of the tower, on your way down the stairs.

HIDDEN POWER-UPS

At the next corner is a doorway. Drop through it to find a large Red Orb. Jump over the low wall blocking the path for another Red Orb, and then jump up the wall onto the shoulder of the massive statue. From the shoulder, jump onto the head and walk around carefully until a cloud of **Bonus Red Orbs** appears out of thin air. There are several locations like this throughout the game. If you see a high ledge or platform anywhere in the game, try to land on it to see if any hidden orbs appear!

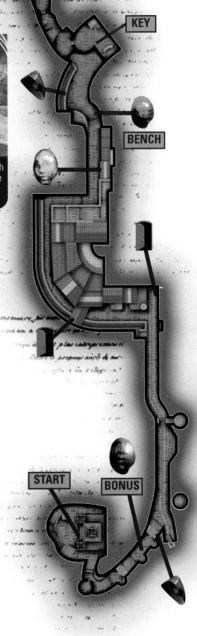

Continuing down the slope, stop under the tall archway. Face the left wall, and press ◎ to begin a Wall Hike. As Dante flips backward off the wall, press ✕ while he is in midair to Air Hike up to the apex of the arch. A **Blue Orb Fragment** hovers near the ceiling, and this method is the only way to propel Dante high enough to reach it.

Jump atop the trolley near the collapsed edge for yet another Red Orb.

ATTACK TERMINOLOGY

You'll notice that we refer to many of Dante's attacks by their proper names. While we always try to hint at how to perform a move, you should review the hero's moves in the Action File. Press **SELECT** to open the Status Menu, choose "File" and select "Action". This helpful in-game tool provides valuable instructions on how to execute most of Dante's cooler moves.

FLIP ESCAPE
AIR HIKE
KICK JUMP
WALL HIKE
HIGH TIME
STINGER
TWOSOME TIME
RAIN STORM
DEVIL TRIGGER

Jump higher than usual by kicking off the wall.

Approach a wall while jumping, hold the left analog stick toward the wall, then press ○ again.

BLUE ORB FRAGMENTS

Blue Orb Fragments are pieces of a complete Blue Orb. When four of these are found, a Blue Orb is instantly formed and the character's vitality meter will be extended. Once the vitality meter reaches its full graphic length, the colors of the meter will double over to reflect the true amount of life energy. Dante and Lucia both start with roughly 60% of a full meter, and the gauge can be lengthened to approximately 200%. Each full Blue Orb increases the vitality meter length by about 10%. Keep your eyes open, because whole Blue Orbs can sometimes be found in the environment as well as purchased through the shops or before the next mission.

SHOW TIME!!!

From the trolley car teetering on the edge, begin the long trek north to the rendezvous with Lucia. Dante steps upon the grizzly scene of several corpses hung from the electric lines in torture devices. Unfortunately, death has not diminished their agony, and they wish to share it with interlopers. Agonofinis are hardly the most dangerous monsters that you'll encounter on the long journey ahead, but neither should they be taken lightly.

AGONOFINIS

Trapped in their torturous cages, these lilting and staggering creatures are hardly a challenge for someone with Dante's arsenal and skills. Encased entirely in metal, they are weak against lightning attacks utilizing the Electro Heart. The most dangerous types are the disc-throwing variety, so eliminate them first whenever Agonofinis are encountered.

Because these creatures are some of the most frail, the chance that they'll be destroyed before a stylish combo can begin is high. Use moves such as **High Time** (Hold ▣ , press the Left Analog Stick away from the enemy, then press △), **Stinger** (Hold ▣ , press the Left Analog Stick toward the enemy, then press △ hard) or a **Spin Bash** (Press △ three times while holding the Left Analog Stick away from the foe's direction) to initiate a stylish combo. Perform more moves to improve the level of the combo, and the exclamation on the right side of the screen will change from "Don't Worry" to "Come On!"

Hard attacks will start a combo. Keep the colored words onscreen to raise the stakes.

If you finish a foe and the next one is far away, keep the combo going by shooting with the Handguns as you move closer.

Eventually you might reach the ultimate "SHOW TIME!!" level, at which point each defeated foe will release up to five times the usual amount of Red

Orbs. Striking stylish combos during every battle is the only way to ensure that you gather Red Orbs fast enough to improve the levels of swords and armaments before the finale of the game. You're graded for your combat prowess during each mission as well!

AERIAL BATTLES

Continue across the bridge into the town, and perform a Wall Hike on the left side to grab a large Red Orb from a gargoyle's mouth high up on the wall. Near the canal, vulture-like demons named Puia materialize and attack. While they are easy enough to blast out of the air with the handguns, they sometimes shoot a missile trio that can hit Dante unexpectedly. Double-jump into the air and begin firing when Dante is on their same level. Remaining airborne for as long as possible while encountering Puia allows Dante to avoid their ground-swoops and projectile attacks.

PUIA

These feathered fiends can fire missiles and swoop down to hit characters on the ground, but they are weak against attacks from the air. Puia are very easy to kill, and only become a nuisance when coupled with stronger types of devils.

SECRET ROOMS

A **Red Orb** hovers over the tall post at the corner, and another sits at the back of the channel, under the bridge. Once they're collected, it's time to visit your first Secret Room. Two Secret Room locations are in the immediate area.

SECRET ROOM LOCATION 1

Move to the large gate just above the channel and, while facing it, press ✕ to enter a Secret Room. Examine the maps at the start of this section for the exact position of the Secret Room location.

SECRET ROOM LOCATION 2

Hop over the low wall dividing the street running alongside the channel, and examine the door on the opposite side to enter the next level Secret Room.

ROOFTOP HOPPING

Proceed up the street along the channel, eliminating groups of Agonofinis that appear. More Red Orbs and enemies can be encountered in a niche formed by the rooftops some distance back from the low wall dividing the street. As you can tell, quick mastery of Kick Jumps and Air Hikes is required to fully explore all the maps.

)The signposts along the street can be smashed to reveal hidden Red Orbs.

A large Red Orb sits on the ledge down in the waterway.

At the back end of a row of balconies, smash two gargoyle statues for Red Orbs, and a nearby park bench for a revitalizing **Green Orb**. Drop down to the street level collect the **Gold Orb** in the middle of the road. Only one Gold Orb can be carried at a time. These items will resurrect Dante automatically with full health and vitality, but they incur a slight penalty in your mission ranking. Stepping into the vicinity of the Gold Orb invites a gruesome battle with several respawning Agonofinis.

THE GOD OF TIME

Around the corner from the street brawl, smash another bench to receive a **Green Orb** if you are damaged, a Red Orb if not. Just beyond that point stands a familiar God of Time statue. Move to the statue and press ✕ to enter the Shop menu. You can use the orbs you've collected to improve the level of weapons, or buy items such as Vital Stars and Devil Stars.

In the drainage passage just below the God of Time Statue is a Blue Orb Fragment!

BATTLE FOR THE KEY

Kick Jump through the high opening in the rounded wall where the Red Orb floats. After a brief cinematic, Dante is locked in a courtyard and must contend with scores of monkey-like devils called Msira. When all the Msira are defeated, the **Key** will drop in the center of the courtyard. Take the Key and move to the iron gate behind which a Red Orb is locked. Dante uses the Key and opens the gate automatically upon touching it.

Tap ☐ rapidly and get those guns blazing. Strike with your sword when close to a Msira to start a stylish combo, and develop the string with gun tricks. To do a gun trick such as **Twosome Time**, lock on to one foe by holding R1. When enemies appear at Dante's back or side, press the Left Analog Stick in that direction and press ☐. Executed with the proper timing and placement of enemies, Dante shoots in two different directions with his guns. Tricks like this can raise the level of the stylish combo, and more Red Orbs will be released per kill.

MSIRA

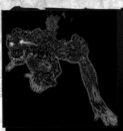

Msira are hunched and misshapen feral demons who lust for blood and chaos. They're more resilient than other types, and several strong sword attacks may be required to strike a stylish combo from one of them. Be prepared to Flip Escape out of the way, because Msira can leap long distances to swipe Dante with their claws.

SMOKESTACK SMASH

Proceed through the crumbling passage into the next section. Continue down the street between the low houses, collecting a string of little Red Orbs. In the clearing at the bottom of the first hill, Dante must contend with an Agonofinis enemy. Once they are defeated, Kick Jump up to the rooftops. Many of the small chimney pipes on the roofs can be smashed for small Red Orbs. When satisfied, move toward the cottage at the top of the area to end the mission.

STRIKING STONES

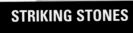

The glowing red stone on the ledge just below the cottage can be struck repeatedly to release a bevy of Red Orbs for Dante to collect. But after a short amount of time, the Striking Stone will cease to glow and yields no more orbs. Slightly more orbs can be gained from the stone by pressing △ three times, pause a split second, then strike three times again, over and over. Basically, you want avoid the final stroke of Dante's normal sword attack, because a long pause follows and you will draw less orbs from the stone.

MISSION COMPLETE!	
S RANK REQUIREMENTS	
CLEAR TIME	8:30 MINUTES
ORBS	3000
STYLISH AVERAGE	4 "SHOW TIME!!" COMBOS
DAMAGE	0
ITEM USED	NONE

MISSION 2

"The summoner bids the hunter to embark upon a fateful quest. Though evil seeks to destroy the outposts of the protectors, a hidden passageway is revealed. In forgotten chambers deep beneath the earth, the hunter will strike at the faces of the old gods to reveal all that which was hidden. Though pitfalls shall plague the hunter, the igniting of the blue flames shall illuminate the path to the gemstone. The aerial heart will give the hunter the chance to reach the skies."

—Guidepost for the Hunters *Chapter 1 Clause 8*

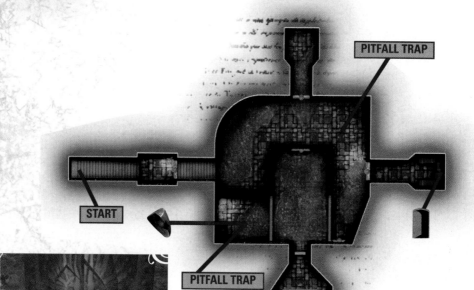

PITFALL TRAP

START

PITFALL TRAP

PITFALL TRAP

STRIKING GLOBE

PITFALL TRAP

DEVIL TRIGGER RECHARGE PLATE

GOD OF TIME

AERIAL HEART

...TIN GODS

Descend the stairs and smash the metal face blocking the passage with Dante's sword. The most efficient method of smashing such tough obstacles is with the Spin Bash. (Press △ repeatedly while holding the Left Analog Stick away from the direction Dante faces.)

Descend the second set of stairs and drop into a vast chamber. Head to Dante's left around a corner, and smash the first metal face you encounter. A hidden passage is revealed. As you move to collect the large Red Orb at the back of the chamber, Dante is ambushed by a set of Agonofinis. Clean them up, exit the passage and continue toward the back of the larger square chamber.

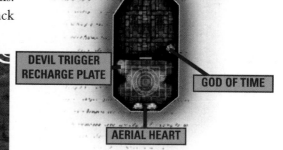

PITFALL TRAPS!

Heading toward the next metal face in the room, Dante may fall into a pit if he steps in the wrong place. Landing at the bottom, several Agonofinis materialize and attack. Be sure to target and destroy the disk-tossing Agonofinis first, to reduce damage received. Try to use Twosome Time gun tricks to keep the others at bay. When the enemies are defeated, Kick Jump out of the pit and continue.

In such a confined area, only quick action and certain tactics will allow the devil hunter to escape unscathed.

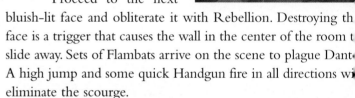
MORE ANCIENT SECRETS

Smash aside the next metal face Dante comes across and proceed into the hidden passage to find a striking stone. Bash the stone for all the orbs it's worth, and examine the open sarcophagus at the back to find a Secret Room.

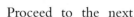

Proceed to the next bluish-lit face and obliterate it with Rebellion. Destroying th face is a trigger that causes the wall in the center of the room t slide away. Sets of Flambats arrive on the scene to plague Dant A high jump and some quick Handgun fire in all directions wi eliminate the scourge.

Although a string of small Red Orbs leads to the exit of the first large chamber, move further around the corner to find another blue-lit face. Smashing this metal plate moves another wall aside in the chamber, revealing - *nothing*. However, if you move into the center of the small area Dante will fall into a harmless pit wherein several Red Orbs and a **Blue Orb Fragment** can be collected.

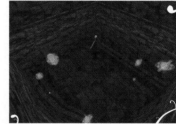

SECRET ROOM LOCATION 1

In the hidden passage where the striking stone is located, move to the open coffin at the back of the room and press ✕ to find the next level Secret Room.

FLAMBAT

These bat-shaped spirits are more annoying than dangerous, but in large groups they can prove deadly. Flambats will dive at the character with a devastating hit. Draining vitality from the victim, they will become larger and more devastating. To avoid multiple hits in succession, jump into the air in the midst of them and shoot the Handguns in rapid-fire style while airborne. One shot should eliminate each Flambat. Since no orbs are released by their extinction, don't try to use sword attacks or spark stylish combos. Just smoke them, and quickly.

TRANSFORMING THE FLAMES

Move across the small connecting chamber and examine the door on the opposite end. The exit is sealed, and if you fail to move away quickly, a large hand will emerge to damage Dante.

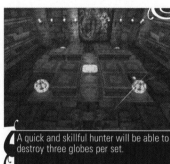

After revealing the seal on the door, a square tile in the middle of the room is lit. Stand on the lit tile to activate a mechanism. The objective is to destroy the glowing globes that appear. Each globe destroyed successfully will change a flame on the back wall from red to blue. When all eight flames have been turned blue, the seal will break and the exit will open.

The situation is complicated, because each set of globes will disappear after just a few seconds. Also, the floor tiles rise in various patterns and restrict access to the globes. As the globes disappear, the tiles will change formations. Jump over the rising tiles from globe to globe. Use the Spin Bash attack to destroy each globe quickly and efficiently. Smash all eight globes to unseal the door, and move on to the next chamber.

A quick and skillful hunter will be able to destroy three globes per set.

COMPLEX CHAMBER

The next chamber is the most complex yet. Proceed to the far side of the room and examine the sealed exit. A clue concerning how to open the door is inscribed. Use the God of Time statue next to the exit to power up if possible.

Return to the first section of the massive room. A bluish-lit face is mounted on the north wall, and a regular face is on the south wall. ***Do not strike the bluish-lit face just yet***, or you'll miss a valuable hidden area. Destroy the face on the south wall, and proceed into the small passage to obtain a **Blue Orb Fragment**. A slow but dangerous creature called a Savage Golem suddenly blocks the exit. Dispatch this monster with all prejudice, and return to the main chamber.

SAVAGE GOLEM

Although extremely tough with doubled vitality meters, these lumbering brutes move extremely slowly. When attacked at close range, they will project long blue spikes tipped with poison to pierce their enemy. They can also extend their limbs under the earth to surprise their prey from underneath with this type of attack. Poison will continuously lower Dante's vitality until either a Holy Star is used or the effect expires. To defeat a Savage Golem, weaken it with constant gunfire. Then use strong sword attacks to hack off the arms and upper torso. When the legs are flung into the corner, things aren't over yet. Lock on to the flailing legs and shoot them until the vitality is wholly depleted, or the monster will regenerate its upper torso and lost limbs and recovering full vitality!

FURTHER ROOM MECHANICS

Smash the blue-lit face on the north wall, and the giant room will be rearranged yet again. In the area revealed to the left of the entrance, smash a new metal face to open a section on the other side of the room. Pyromancers casting fire spells materialize and try to turn up the heat. While these evil magicians are not hard to dispatch, there is a pit fall in the new area of the room where more Savage Golems wait to attack. Avoid the pitfall trap until the Pyromancers are neutralized.

If caught in the pit between both types of enemies at once, things could get ugly.

PYROMANCER

For a swift dead shot like Dante, spell-casting wizards are truly outdated opponents. Because of their short vitality bars and frail bodies, Pyromancers are easily chopped up and perforated. The only way to strike a stylish combo against a set of Pyromancer enemies is to stand in one place and wait for them to teleport closer to Dante. Use a strong sword attack to spark a stylish combo, then maintain and increase the combo with gunfire and Twosome Time. If a Pyromancer begins to cast gouts of flame, stay out of range and interrupt their attack by shooting.

Destroy the metal god in the new area to reveal a short corridor. Inside of this passage is a striking globe, a type of key object encountered frequently. Continue striking the globe with Dante's sword until all of the squares encircling it are changed from white to purple. If you wait too long between attacks, the squares will soon change back to white. When a ring is formed around the globe, the seal on the exit door next to the God of Time statue will be broken.

Spin Bash attacks (Press ⓐ three times while holding the Left Analog Stick away from target) work most quickly against the globe.

SECRET ROOM LOCATION 2

Examine the open standing sarcophagus to the left of the striking globe to discover the next Secret Room.

30

THE AERIAL HEART

The final chamber of the underground houses a contest of devil versus devil. On the far wall is a sealed window, inside which lies the Aerial Heart. To unseal the Amulet Stone, you must defeat three enemy sets in the room. The first batch is a group of Agonofinis, two of which are disk-whipping monsters. Then a group of Pyromancers must be defeated. Unfortunately, the two statues on top of the altar will come to life and attack. One Goatling drops to the ground while the other shoots homing missiles from the air. Don't be afraid to use your Devil Trigger power, because there is a DT Recharge Plate in the corner near the entrance. Only when the Goatlings are defeated can the **Aerial Heart** be obtained.

The Aerial Heart is automatically equipped in the Amulet. Recharge Dante's Devil Trigger to full using the recharge plate in the corner, then Devil Trigger (L1) and fly up to the ceiling. Grab the orbs and fly into the doorway high above to end the mission.

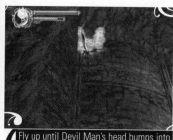

Fly up until Devil Man's head bumps into the corner of the ceiling near the exit to release **Bonus Red Orbs**.

GOATLING

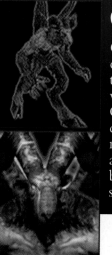

Goatlings are strong enemies that have some flight ability. On the ground, they charge at Dante and attempt to bash him aside with powerful claw swipes. The best technique for fighting a Goatling on the ground is to shoot it until it begins to convulse, then bash it off its feet with a powerful sword attack such as the Spin Bash. Once it's down, keep it from getting back up with continuous gunfire or sword chops. While hovering in air, a Goatling will charge and release powerful homing missiles that Dante must dodge using jumps or the Flip Escape (●). Dante is weak against this attack if he jumps up to the Goatling's level, so stay on the ground and blast the creature out of the sky with a barrage of bullets. Multiple Goatlings make survival extremely difficult, so good luck.

MISSION COMPLETE!	
S RANK REQUIREMENTS	
CLEAR TIME	6:30 MINUTES
ORBS	3000
STYLISH AVERAGE	2 "SHOW TIME!!" COMBOS
DAMAGE	0
ITEM USED	NONE

MISSION 3

"Though the Bridge of Sighs is fallen, the hunter can find an alternate path into the hideous city. From the door to death's catacombs, the hunter need only find the key to heaven's gate. The key to the next journey begins and ends with death. But the hungry one clings tightly to the object of desire."

-Guidepost for the Hunters *Chapter 2 Clause 4*

BACK ON THE STREETS

Emerge from the starting alley to a Y-shaped intersection. Kick Jump up the wall at the junction to capture three Red Orbs. Continue moving towards the screen in order to engage a large group of Agonofinis. A large Red Orb hovers over the large gate at the end.

Jump on top of both large columns to unleash **2 Bonus Red Orb** locations!

Although someone has destroyed the bridge to Uroboros City, a **Blue Orb Fragment** hides on the left side!

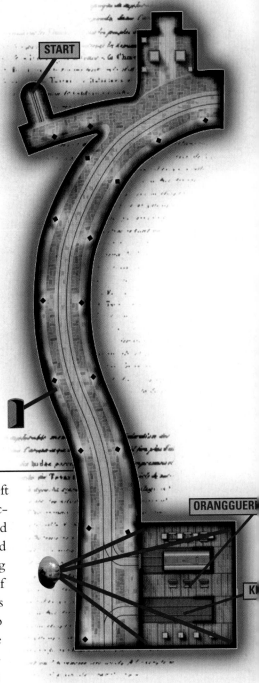

THE GOATLING'S GAUNTLET

Head down the left branch of the Y-intersection, until Dante is sealed inside the zone by a red barrier. A special Goatling hovering at the bottom of the street will cause clouds of demonic energy to erupt from under Dante until he reaches the floating foe and brings it down.

Run down the street toward the Goatling, ignoring Agonofinis enemies as well as Red Orbs hovering over several of the streetlights. The best method to avoid the exploding energy is to run in a zigzag pattern toward the Goatling, from the left side of the street to the right. Look for shadows forming on the ground, warning of imminent energy explosions.

If Dante cannot run out of the way in time, use the Flip Escape ⊙ to nullify damage while he is rolling.

Once Dante is extremely close to the Goatling, attack the beast as usual and the ground will stop exploding. The death of the Goatling permanently removes all the enemies from the area, and unseals the massive doors of the trolley station.

"Though the Bridge of Sighs is fallen, the hunter can find an alternate path into the hideous city. From the door to death's catacombs, the hunter need only find the key to heaven's gate. The key to the next journey begins and ends with death. But the hungry one clings tightly to the object of desire."

-Guidepost for the Hunters *Chapter 2 Clause 4*

THE QUIET, EMPTY STREET

Now you should head back up the street and collect the Red Orbs floating above four of the streetlights. The exit, locked by angelic iron gates, requires a key. Collect the two Red Orbs to either side of it and enter the trolley station to find that key.

Use the God of Time Statue across the street from the trolley station entrance to power up if possible.

SECRET ROOM LOCATION 1

Check this almost nondescript door on the right side of the street to find a Secret Room, before entering the trolley station for the boss fight.

ORANGGUERRA

RECOMMENDED SWORD	REBELLION
RECOMMENDED GUN	HANDGUNS
RECOMMENDED AMULET	AERIAL HEART, ELECTRO HEART

Unfortunately, Dante has yet to collect the weapons and Amulet Stones that are best suited for fighting this monster. The recommended equipment reflects only Dante's available items during a first game. Keep in mind for a replay game that the Orangguerra is actually weak versus cold attacks, and the Shotgun is the best gun to use.

During your first encounter with Orangguerra, you have quite a battle on your hands. The creature's worst attack is being able to leap out of camera view, and swiftly land on Dante's head. Whenever the creature leaps up, you can't be sure whether it's going to pounce on the devil hunter and flatten him or use the ceiling as a set of monkey bars to climb around the station. Either way, whenever the creature flies off the ground the safest thing to do is execute one or more Flip Escapes ⬤ until the Orangguerra crashes to the ground.

The safest thing to do is place as much distance between Orangguerra and Dante as possible, and keep shooting until his Devil Trigger gauges are fully charged. Unfortunately, the creature will also fire large force balls at Dante when the range is long. Luckily, there are quite a few obstacles in the room, which Dante can dart behind and use for cover. However, almost everything in the room is breakable, and Orangguerra loves to smash things that get in the way.

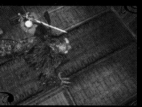

There are some instances when the rabid monster gets so caught up in the chaos that it seems to lose track of Dante, and these are opportunities to exploit. Run directly at the creature, then Flip Escape to the left or right. Position Dante directly behind the creature, and try to inflict one or two really strong sword attacks before it can turn or leap away. The trick to powering up those Devil Trigger gauges faster is to use sword attacks, but unfortunately staying in close range of Orangguerra is really difficult and dangerous. Use the **Green Orbs** in the corners of the room to keep Dante healthy after each major hit he absorbs.

Once those Devil Trigger gauges are fully charged, it's time to end this battle. Jump into the air and fly, but maintain a low altitude. Basically, you want to steer the floating Devil Man at the creature's head. Press ▲ while flying to perform Dante's Round Trip attack, and his sword will score multiple hits as it boomerangs around the big ape's head. Perform this attack a few times, and the boss's vitality gauge will be greatly reduced. If Orangguerra manages to escape while Dante is in Devil Trigger, then press ⬤ to fire little lightning bursts at the monster with submachine gun speed. If you run out of Devil Trigger before the monster is dead, then keep shooting with guns and performing hit-and-run strikes with the sword until Dante's DT gauge is just above the first line. Then Devil Trigger again and you should be able to easily finish off this King Kong wannabe.

THE GATES OF HEAVEN

When defeated, Orangguerra drops the **Key** for the angelic gates. Grab the item and the Red Orbs left by the vanquished foe, and exit the trolley station. The only thing left to do is unlock the gates in front of the massive door on the street outside, and exit.

MISSION COMPLETE!	
S RANK REQUIREMENTS	
CLEAR TIME	8:30 MINUTES
ORBS	4500
STYLISH AVERAGE	6 "SHOW TIME!!" COMBOS
DAMAGE	0
ITEM USED	NONE

MISSION 4

"Near the water's edge lies the lair of a water demoness. To enter her domain, the hunter must acquire new levels of speed. She has many arms but only one heart, as she waits for the hunter deep in the water."

-Guidepost for the Hunters *Chapter 4 Clause 5*

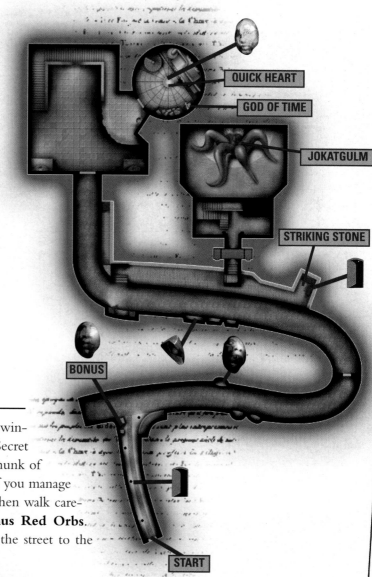

QUICK HEART

GOD OF TIME

JOKATGULM

STRIKING STONE

BONUS

START

SECRET ROOM LOCATION 1

Just a few doors down the slope from the starting point, search the window on the right side of the street to find a Secret Room.

TOP OF THE ALLEY

Move down the sloping street, and check the windows on the right side of the screen to find a Secret Room. Kick Jump up the wall on the to a broken chunk of archway hanging high above to collect a Red Orb. If you manage to jump from this ledge to the one farther up, and then walk carefully out to the edge, you'll release a cloud of **Bonus Red Orbs**. Another Red Orb can be gained by leaping across the street to the edge on the opposite corner.

Push the Left Analog Stick very lightly so that Dante walks slowly on the ledge to trigger the Bonus Red Orbs.

DESCENT TO THE HARBOR

Kick Jump to the top of the door at the north end of the curved and sloping street for another Red Orb. Proceed down the slope to encounter a batch of Msira. Although a second cluster waits near the wall at the bottom of the hill,

jump high along the cliffs on the right hand wall to find a Red Orb. A whole **Blue Orb** is on a ledge hanging over the left side of the street.

Defeat the group of Msira guarding the barricade in front of a massive wall at the bottom of the hill. Smash the wooden obstruction by attacking repeatedly with Rebellion, and continue under the wall to the harbor area.

POINTS ALONG THE SEAWALLS

Running along the curving slope, begin jumping along the wall on the left side. Jump up to grab a small Red Orb on the lowest ledge, and then jump straight up to the next surface. Carefully Kick Jump off the cliff face to reach another small Red Orb on the ledge to the upper right. Then Kick Jump off the rock wall straight upward to reach a **Blue Orb Fragment**.

Move across the street and drop over a small embankment. Collect a row of Red Orbs lined up along the bank wall on the docks, and head up the small set of steps. The gate to the boss fight area is closed. Surely there must be a way to open it?

Continue along the dock past the closed gate to the end, where a striking stone is found. After bashing the glowing rock for all the Red Orbs it's worth, check the garage door nearby to find a Secret Room.

SECRET ROOM LOCATION 2

Check the garage door near the striking stone at the south end of the dock area to find a Secret Room.

GLIMMER OF THE LIGHTHOUSE

Hop along the buildings near the cliff face to find Red Orbs, and Kick Jump up to the scaffold above the tarps to collect more. Near the entrance to the lighthouse is an object that can be struck to open the gate in the center of the dock. However, the gate will close before Dante can reach it. There must be some solution to your dilemma inside the coastal safety signal building.

Defeat a group of Agonofinis to unseal the door on the level above. Inside the small lighthouse mechanics room, you will find the gem that is the source of illumination here: The **Quick Heart**. When equipped in Dante's Amulet, this stone enables him to move at amazing speeds while in Devil Trigger.

  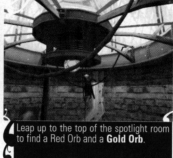

After receiving the Quick Heart, Air Hike to the top of the chamber to receive a **Gold Orb**.

Leap up to the top of the spotlight room to find a Red Orb and a **Gold Orb**.

LAIR OF THE WATER DEVIL

While exiting the lighthouse, defeat as many Agonofinis as are required to fill Dante's Devil Trigger gauges. The only way you are going to make it through the gate and defeat the boss in the next area is with every once of power of which Dante is capable.

Strike the globe just outside the lighthouse until it glows, and the gate on the docks opens. As soon as you regain control of Dante, Devil Trigger and run over to the stairs leading down to the docks. Dash across the docks and through the gate before it drops too low to allow Dante to pass.

Don't jump or try to fly while running for the gate, it only slows you down!

To the right inside the gate is a Green Orb. Take it even if you don't need your health replenished, and it will be added to your Red Orb count. Concealed on a ledge above the doorway is a Red Orb. Collect these and enter the door to encounter another boss.

JOKATGULM

RECOMMENDED SWORD	REBELLION
RECOMMENDED GUN	HANDGUNS
RECOMMENDED AMULET	QUICK HEART, ELECTRO HEART

Again, Dante does not have the best equipment to defeat this Devil. When replaying the game, keep in mind that Jokatgulm is weak versus fire, and that the Shotgun is the best weapon to use against the tentacles while the Merciless sword inflicts the best damage against the body stem.

Damage is only inflicted to Jokatgulm by attacking the central body stem, which is guarded by four tentacles. At least one of the tentacles must be eliminated to be able to attack the body at all. The tentacle will respawn in roughly 10 seconds, so that doesn't leave much time to inflict damage. If you're standing inside the tentacles when all four are active the Jokatgulm will erect a shield, which knocks Dante away from the monster.

Most of the battle will be spent dealing with the tentacles. Position Dante near the wall at the outside of the area, and tap ⚪ quickly to pump Handgun bullets rapid fire at one or two tentacles. Rather than try to fight all the appendages, just stay to one side of the creature so that only one or two limbs are actively seeking to damage Dante. As tentacles sweep left and right attempting to hit the devil hunter,

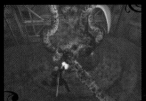 

jump once and only once to evade them. Fire rapidly while Dante is in the air. As he starts to come down, you can press ❌ again to Air Hike and keep him aloft to avoid damage. There are a few instances where tentacles will curl upward. If they have been damaged quite a bit already by gunfire, you can get under them and quickly sever them with a few sword chops.

When one or more tentacles are destroyed, land and Devil Trigger. Run toward the creature as fast as possible, assisted by the Quick Heart stone. Jump onto the central shell and attack the body stem with Rebellion.

Unfortunately, the body defends itself by spewing a poison gas cloud. Poisoning will reduce Dante's vitality for several seconds after the first hit, but if you want a chance at damaging the monster, it's almost unavoidable. Try to stay on the side of the creature where you entered, so that when the tentacles re-spawn you can see them and leap away safely. Resume blasting the tentacles until one disappears, then repeat this process. Several assaults in this manner will be required to end the battle.

It may take longer to defeat the boss, but you can avoid damage simply by staying back from the body stem and shooting instead. When a tentacle dies, Devil Trigger and run forward. Move back and forth until the body stem is targeted, then hold R1 to lock on and fire. The insanely fast pounding should eventually get the best of it. This way, you can avoid all damage if you're going for an S ranking for the mission.

DADDY GETS A BOOM STICK

Collect the bevy of Red Orbs left by the water demon and enter the garage that opens on the right side of the area. Dante finds a new weapon, the **Shotgun**, and after a short daredevil stunt, the mission is over.

MISSION COMPLETE!	
S RANK REQUIREMENTS	
CLEAR TIME	9:30 MINUTES
ORBS	5000
STYLISH AVERAGE	8 "SHOW TIME!!" COMBOS
DAMAGE	0
ITEM USED	NONE

MISSION 5

"Desolate are the city streets borne of evil's will. Death's ancient knight sends his familiars to test the will of the hunter. The path is opened through death, but guarded still by foes thought vanquished. Fear the machinations of mankind, for easily can they be brought into the service of hatred. A whirling winged one pursues the hunter high into the sky. Close to your eyes, but far off in your mind, the hunter must learn the value of options. Though the enemy stands in the path, escape is wiser than conflict."

-Guidepost for the Hunters *Chapter 5 Clause 4*

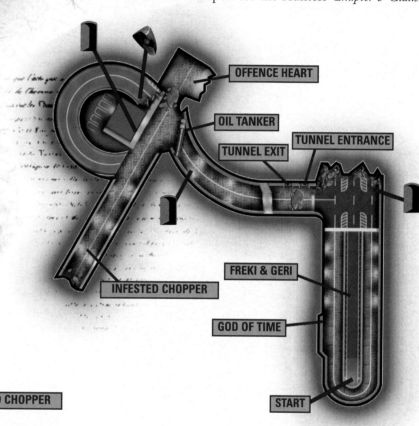

OFFENCE HEART

OIL TANKER

TUNNEL EXIT

TUNNEL ENTRANCE

INFESTED CHOPPER

FREKI & GERI

GOD OF TIME

START

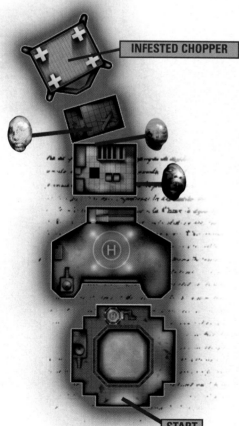

INFESTED CHOPPER

START

WHITE WOLF PHANTOMS

Just ahead of Dante is a Red Orb on the right side of the tunnel. While attempting to exit the underground passage, Dante finds himself barred by an ephemeral barrier. Two white wolves named Freki and Geri materialize and attack. Tough monsters, they will take and administer quite a bit of punishment before fleeing.

Lure the wolves to the corners, then Devil Trigger and cleave them up!

The best strategy for dealing with these monsters is to position Dante in a corner of the square area. As the creatures attempt to charge at the red-cloaked one, jump straight up and tap the ⬜ button rapidly to inundate them with lead. When Dante's empty Devil Trigger gauges finally reach the first or second line, press 🔳 when both wolves are directly under him and use strong sword attacks to try to kill one or both. Dante will not be released from the tunnel exit until both wolves are reunited with their master high atop the Uroboros towers.

HARDLY CATCH A BREATH...

Freed from the trap of the white wolves, proceed out of the tunnel to the street surface only to be greeted by a difficult set of Puia and Goatlings. Jump over the guardrails to keep the charging goat demons at bay while Dante sinks the air raiders. Dispatch the horned giants with powerful sword attacks and rapid fire Handgun blasts.

A God of Time statue stands in a niche on the raised sidewalk along the west wall.

Red Orbs can be obtained at the curved lip of the tunnel entrance as well as over the sidewalk at the bottom of the area.

Eliminate another set of the same, and the barriers surrounding the area will be removed. Now you can finally explore the area and discover what may lurk around every corner. When finished, enter the tunnel indicated when the last enemy set fell.

SECRET ROOM LOCATION 1

Though there are many doors along the raised sidewalk, the one at the top corner leads to a Secret Room. Refer to the maps for this mission to get the specific location.

BLOOD GOAT

A taller, stronger and more resilient version of Goatlings, these evil ceremonial monsters can remain in the air longer, and won't hesitate to pelt devil hunters with multiple homing missiles. The same tactics used to defeat their weaker siblings also work for this type, but it's a good idea to weaken them up a little with gunfire before attempting to knock them flat with sword attacks.

MONKEY MASTER

Proceed along the next section of city street until your old pal Orangguerra reappears, along with a half dozen flaming monkey demons known as Homromsira. The apelike devil appears here as a regular enemy, and though it has a full green vitality bar the Orangguerra actually has only the same amount of life. Use the same tactics as described in the previous boss fight for Mission 3, except use the Shotgun against Orangguerra for much quicker results.

Try to bait the Orangguerra into bashing the Homromsira by mistake! You won't get Red Orbs for the fire monkeys, but it's amusing!

HOMROMSI

Fire versions of Msira enemies, these particular foes are not much different than their cousins. They are weak against cold attacks and have a higher vitality than most other Msira types. The intense heat of their bodies makes their attacks more devastating.

SECRET ROOM LOCATION 2

Before leaping over the derelict oil truck at the end of the street, leap up to the raised sidewalk and examine the door on the left side of the street to find a Secret Room. Check our maps in this mission section for better clarification.

THE INFESTED TANKS

Jumping over the oil tanker blocking the road, Dante comes face to face with the horror of the Infestants, demons who can possess people and machines. In this case, the demons have taken over three military tanks in the area. The target and weak spot of Infested Tanks is an eyeball on top of the rotating turret on each tank. Unfortunately, standing anywhere on top of a tank is dangerous due to the machine gun mounted nearby, which will blast Dante off the top. Dust off the two armored monstrosities on the ground level, then ascend the ramp and take out the final tank.

BLAST CRAZY

On the street level, standing between the two tanks and dashing out of the way just in time may cause the two tanks to crossfire, causing massive damage to one another!

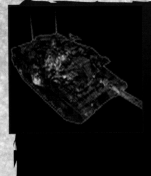

INFESTED TANK

For true effectiveness against the possessed military tanks patrolling the Uroboros city sector, Dante must attack from above. Jump onto the turret and blast the eyeball target with the Handguns or shotguns. However, do not remain standing on the turret or there is danger of being hit by the heavy machinegun mounted near the cockpit hatch. When the Devil Trigger gauges glow, use the Aerial Heart stone to fly above them and fire electric bolts at the eyeball. Infested tanks are weak against the effects of the Electro Heart while Dante is in Devil Trigger.

RUINED ENTRANCE RAMP AND OFFENCE HEART

Defeating the last Infested Tank on the highway entrance ramp, continue running to the top of the ramp to find a Red Orb and a **Blue Orb Fragment**. Drop from the broken edge to the macadam far below.

Jump onto the rubble near the burning oil truck, and leap over the debris to find an area that is practically hidden. Behind the full-scale fencing is another Amulet Stone altar, where Dante obtains the **Offence Heart**. Boosting the power of attacks while Dante is in Devil Trigger mode, you will certain need the assistance of this stone in the battle to come…

There's a lone Red Orb to collect in the back corner of a parking lot under the ramp.

SECRET ROOM LOCATION 3

When the Infested Tanks are dismantled, enter the cathedral-like doors on the building within the curl of the highway ramp to find the next Secret Room.

HELICOPTER ALERT!

When finished collecting Orbs and items in the city area, move past the start of the highway ramp, and continue down the street until an Infested Helicopter flies upon the scene and attacks Dante.

The Infested Chopper will chase Dante through the buildings and rooftops for the next several areas, until Dante reaches the zone where the official boss fight begins. Each incarnation of the Infested Chopper has a separate vitality gauge, and if depleted the flying machine will leave Dante alone until he reaches the next area. However, you gain no Red Orbs or boss bonus by defeating any of the Infested Chopper appearances except for the final stage. Bear in mind, while you are engaging all forms of the Helicopter, that until you reach the boss fight, all combat with it is entirely optional.

For instance, in the first battle where the helicopter has blown up the wall of the building and created a gaping hole, you only need to enter the building to escape the chopper for the moment. If you do stay on the street and confront the possessed aircraft, there is no bonus or reward. There is only the possibility of lowering your mission score by wasting time and taking damage.

INFESTED CHOPPER

This military grade attack helicopter is fitted with a swiveling machine gun on the nose, twin rocket launchers under each wing and two lock-on target tracking ballistic missiles that will follow Dante through the air and across the ground. The target and weak point of the demonic chopper is the large eyeball on the rear of the right side of the craft. The other portions of the ship are still made mostly of metal, and are invulnerable to gunfire. When fighting an Infested Helicopter, try to position Dante off to the right side of the ship so that he is hitting the eyeball directly. Infested Choppers are weak against electric Devil Trigger attacks, so equip the Electro Heart.

THE TOWERING INFERNO

Once inside the building lobby, run behind the first column on the left to gather a Red Orb. More Red Orbs can be obtained on the edges of the balconies just above the main stairs. Start jumping from level to level, working your way up inside the building.

Around the point where Dante reaches the fourth story, the lobby becomes consumed in flames and the Infested Chopper reappears. Ignore both events and continue jumping up to higher levels. Equip the Aerial Heart, so that if you're having trouble reaching the next platform up, all you have to do is Devil Trigger and fly to the point you can't reach. If you land on a bridge or balcony and there doesn't seem to be a level above you, run across the bridge and continue around the level until the next ledge appears above.

The top level inside the blazing building is different than the rest. Except for the area directly in front of the exit, there is only a thin ledge running around the ceiling. The easiest way to reach is to stand Dante facing the balcony rail, then double jump. Timed correctly, the second jump will result in a back flip, and Dante will land on the edge. The Helicopter attacks furiously at this point, so quickly run around the ledge to the exit door.

ROOFTOP HOP

Arriving on the roof of the gutted inferno that used to be an attractive professional building, Dante watches the Infested Chopper rise through the collapsed ceiling. Run all the way around the roof and leap onto the helicopter-landing

pad. Touch the back of the landing pad, and Dante will leap to the next building.

Don't miss the Red Orbs on the lower balcony, situated at either end of this building. Jump onto the roof and leap onto the scaffold between buildings for a Red Orb. There is another Red Orb to be collected on the left side of the building's architecture, and then you should start leaping

upward from ledge to ledge. Puia will materialize and attack, but you can just ignore them until Dante reaches higher levels. Shooting from above, he can easily take out these unwanted intruders in the contest between the devil hunter and the Infested Chopper.

Reaching the level just below the roof on this building, move to the right side and hop into the winch lift. The platform will drop, allowing Dante to regain and extend his vitality by grabbing a complete **Blue Orb**. Kick Jump back up to the ledge, and then flip onto the roof. Run and leap off the back of the rooftop in such a manner as to collect a **Green Orb** and three Red Orbs on your descent to the next building's top.

WHERE EAGLES DARE

Tucked in a small alcove on the roof covered with construction materials is a **Gold Orb**. Collect it even if you already have one, for a bonus to your Red Orb stockpile. Jump onto the beam next to the golden building, and then jump on the ledge. Dante must Kick Jump carefully from one eagle's head to the next on the curved side of the building. Naturally, more Puia try to make things difficult. Height is tantamount so try to jump up a few more levels before contending with these flying pests. Reaching the top level of the building, the Infested Chopper reappears for the true battle.

On the backside of the structure is another set of eagle heads you can use to ascend the building, where the camera angle is less severe.

44

INFESTED CHOPPER

RECOMMENDED SWORD	REBELLION
RECOMMENDED GUN	HANDGUNS
RECOMMENDED AMULET	AERIAL HEART, ELECTRO HEART, OFFENCE HEART

Three plus-shaped (+) towers stand at each corner of the building's roof, and these are the key points from which to attack this persistent pestilence. Pound the chopper with a constant barrage of Handgun fire. Tapping □ rapidly, use your instincts to spot a good moment to Kick Jump onto one of the raised corners. Try to jump on a corner where Dante will be positioned beside or just under the eyeball target on the rear right side of the helicopter.

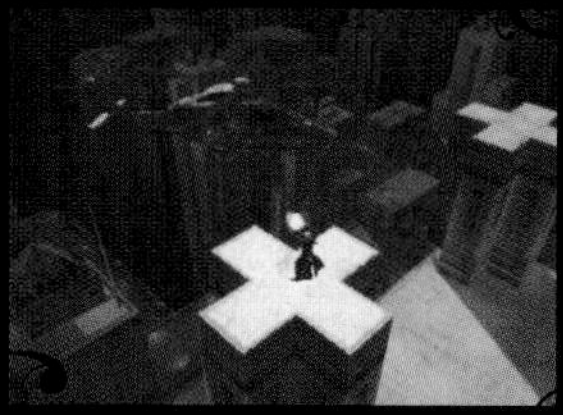

Remain on the plus-shaped platform until the helicopter fires. Leap over machinegun bullets and land on the raised corner to continue firing. Make sure to Flip Escape off of the raised level if the helicopter fires rockets or the lock-on missiles. When chased by missiles, attempt to lead them into the sides of the raised corners, or target and blast them with Handgun fire when they dive to Dante's standing level.

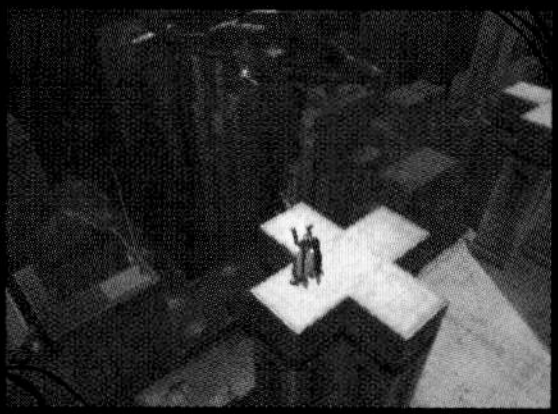

Once the Devil Trigger gauges are full, Air Hike up from one of the raised corners as high as possible, fly at the eyeball on the side of the helicopter, and spray it with the Devil Man's lightning fire attack □. However, there is a danger in jumping too high, because the helicopter's most devastating attack occurs completely by accident; if Dante hits the propeller blades of the helicopter, he will be flung to the ground. Both hits do a tremendous amount of damage, so gauge your distance from the chopper wisely before any jumps.

This really is all the strategy you can use to defeat the chopper. The main challenge is that the target is so high in the air most of the time that it's very hard to inflict massive amounts of damage with sword attacks, as you're more familiar with by now. The only way to spark a stylish combo while fighting the Infested Helicopter is by narrowly dodging one of its projectiles. Just keep your thumb tapping the □, Devil Trigger whenever possible, and this battle will be over in a short while.

MISSION COMPLETE!

S RANK REQUIREMENTS

CLEAR TIME	11:30 MINUTES
ORBS	6000
STYLISH AVERAGE	12 "SHOW TIME!!" COMBOS
DAMAGE	0
ITEM USED	NONE

MISSION 6

"The city of evil is not constructed by the hands of man. The very materials are the bones and sinews of an ancient demon, conjured and summoned to be the brickwork for the sorcerer's schemes. The hunter has left the city derelict, and so the ancient awakens. Its extremities reach the sky. Its intestines reflect the color of darkness. Its name means a tower of misery. The hunter has discovered the deep root of evil."

-Guidepost for the Hunters *Chapter 6 Clause 2*

THE BUILDING ATTACKS!

Use the God of Time statue if desired, and then head toward the top of the city block to engage a new monstrous creation.

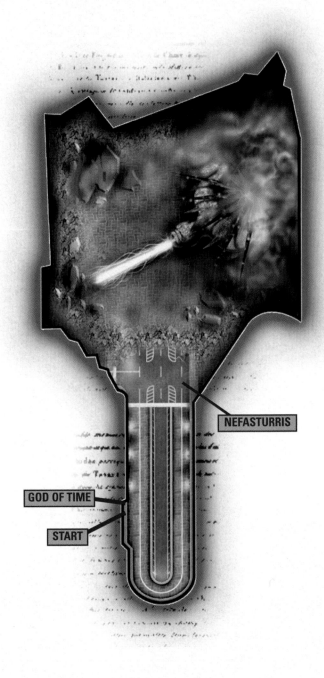

NEFASTURRIS, NEFASVERMIS

RECOMMENDED SWORD	REBELLION
RECOMMENDED GUN	HANDGUNS
RECOMMENDED AMULET	QUICK HEART, ELECTRO HEART, OFFENCE HEART

Air Hike over the Nefasturris's mouth beam attack, and Flip Escape whenever it fires a star-pattern spread of projectiles. Tap the ⬤ button rapidly to saturate the head with bullets, whether you're on the ground or leaping over mouth beam attacks.

After most of its first vitality bar is gone, the massive mutant will dig deep within the earth and release a swarm of the bat-like creatures called Nefasvermis. If you approach too closely to the main boss, these can attack and even knock you to the ground. But also, when you approach the flock and fire the Shotgun, several of them will burst and release Red Orbs. This is the easiest way to reach your Orb requirement to get an S for this mission. If you desire to focus solely on the main boss, jump around until Dante targets the Nefasturris's head, and hold R1 to lock on.

NEFASCAPITIS

RECOMMENDED SWORD	REBELLION
RECOMMENDED GUN	HANDGUNS
RECOMMENDED AMULET	QUICK HEART, ELECTRO HEART, OFFENCE HEART

Keep blasting the attacking the living building until the head is decapitated from the body. Dash toward the skull, firing and dodging spread-projectile attacks, until you reach the neck vertebrates extending from the rear of the skull. Attack the neck and back of the head with hard sword attacks, and Devil Trigger to strengthen your blows.

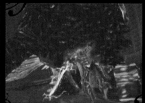

If the Nefascapitis floats away, turn off Devil Trigger and dodge it's attacks while following it. As the mouth fires large white energy balls, perform Flip Escapes ⬤ to the left or right. As soon as the head lands on the ground, Devil Trigger again and quickly run to the rear of the cranium. Slash away at the neck stem while in Devil Trigger, and continue slashing even if Dante's superpower expires.

When the Nefascapitis dies, it drops a pile of Red Orbs directly under it. Because the mission ends immediately, Dante must be standing directly under the monster when it croaks in order to receive any orbs for this villain. Watch the monster's vitality gauge closely and when it gets down to that last little bit, hold off on the gunfire and use only sword attacks.

MISSION COMPLETE!	
S RANK REQUIREMENTS	
CLEAR TIME	8:00 MINUTES
ORBS	1000
STYLISH AVERAGE	10 "SHOW TIME!!" COMBOS
DAMAGE	0
ITEM USED	NONE

MISSION 7

"Evil's source is a wellspring of electric energy, drawn from the demon world and harnessed in steel and concrete. The hunter must enter the structure and acquire the tools crafted by the demons, in order to defeat them. A perilous ride through a deep passage in the earth shall guide the hunter to his destiny. A meeting of power shall end in conflict."

-Guidepost for the Hunters *Chapter 7 Clause 1*

POWER PLANT ENTRANCE

Emerge from the entry niche, head around the right corner and check the shutter door to discover the problem with this power plant; there's no power. Drop to the lower floor to fight a large set of Msira and Homromsira, then Kick Jump up the other wall to the door at the top. Step onto the slanted pipe, and Dante will slide out of the room, collecting Red Orbs along the way.

Build up your Devil Trigger gauges against the monkey demons. You'll need speed to accomplish the next task.

Blast a flock of Puia out of the sky as you work your way to the door at the bottom of the outdoor area between buildings.

Hidden between four tall objects near the west wall is a **Gold Orb**.

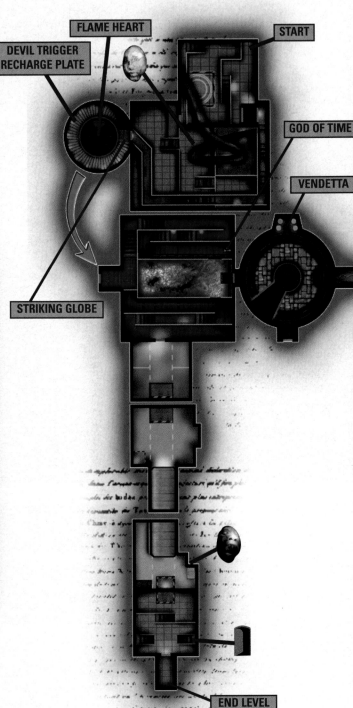

Map labels: FLAME HEART, START, DEVIL TRIGGER RECHARGE PLATE, GOD OF TIME, VENDETTA, STRIKING GLOBE, END LEVEL

48

THE DOWNWARD SPIRAL

Strike the globe near the top entrance until a force field is removed from a gemstone inside the core of the tower. Equip the Quick Heart and then Devil Trigger. Dash down the spiral stairs at lightning speed, and ignore the enemy sets

that materialize. The Agonofinis appearing on the stairs will be accompanied by bomb demons called Spiceres. If Dante gets too close to these or shoots them, they'll explode and damage Dante as well as destroy the enemies. Don't waste your time; just run for the bottom.

Grab the Red Orb in front of the door at the bottom, but don't exit just yet. Continue to the very end of the spiral, where a Devil Trigger Recharge Plate sits. Step on it and refill Dante's gauges, then enter the core of the silo. Grab the large Red Orb at the bottom, then equip the Aerial Heart, transform into Devil Trigger mode, and fly to the top of the inner cylinder to obtain the **Flame Heart**. Dante can now use the power of fire in his Devil Trigger attacks. Drop

to the bottom of the shaft, use the Recharge Plate once again, and enter the greenish-lit door just a few yards back in the spiral.

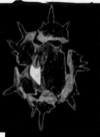

SPICERE

Luckily these floating orbs of self-destructing death will be rarely encountered, because they detonate when Dante is in the proximity or when they're fired upon. Any other enemy types in range of the blast are destroyed, without releasing any Red Orbs. Whenever Spiceres are encountered in enemy groups, the best you can hope for is to annihilate the whole group by destroying the Spicere, and that Dante won't get caught in the blast.

THE MAGMA CHAMBER

Defeat a set of Flambats and Homromsira, who are right at home in the environs of a boiling hot magma pit. Use the God of Time Statue at the bottom platform. Quickly jump from the side of the magma pit to a tiny platform in the center.

SECRET OF THE FLAME HEART

Low on vitality? Equip the Flame Heart, press ⓛ to Devil Trigger, and stand in the magma pit for a while. Dante will absorb all fire damage, meaning that the magma will actually **heal** him!

SECRET ROOM LOCATION 1

Jump across the magma pit, on the far side across from the entrance. Move Dante into the bottom corner beside the stairs (kitty corner from the God of Time), and check to find a Secret Room location. This is certainly a location you could easily miss.

SWORD OF VENGEANCE

Enter the door on the small brick platform just above the surface of the magma. Stabbed into an unfortunate torture victim is the broadsword **Vendetta**, which is excellent to use against large enemies or hard-shelled devils.

DEVIL DESCENDING

Return to the magma chamber and jump to the right side of the room. In the middle of the top platform stands a door leading to a lift. Jump on the platform to begin a slow descent. Flambats plague your trip on the way down, and Blood Goats will attack as the lift nears the bottom. Use the guardrail of the lift platform as an obstacle between you and the big brutes. If they jump inside the rail, jump off the lift and attack from outside!

Before stepping on the elevator lift, Air Hike up to the ceiling of the room to snag two large Red Orbs.

A large Red Orb is hidden in the alcove on the left side of the train.

DEATH TRAIN

Enter the train, and a long ride to the Oil Field begins. Msira and Terreofinis flood the compartment. All of the objects in the train car are breakable, so swing that sword left and right. You should easily be able to complete one or more "Show Time!!" combos before the train docks at the Oil Field's sublevel.

TERREOFINIS

Hopefully you've been improving the strength of your weapons, because the tougher and more sinister brothers of the Agonofinis just showed up. Most are armed with the same type of weapons, and unarmed Terreofinis are going to attempt their "possession" attack more often. Don't let the devil hunter get sucked inside those cages. Like other metal-encased foes, Terreofinis are weak versus electric attacks.

50

ARRIVAL

When the train finally stops, exit through the door on the far side. Smash the crates to the right of the train for several Red Orbs. Hop onto the large, unbreakable crate and Kick Jump up the wall to the high corner of the room. A whole **Blue Orb** is hidden on a ledge high above the floor.

Jump onto the lift to activate Dante's rise to the top. Stand against the front rail as the devil hunter ascends, and jump high into the air to collect Red Orbs en route. Flambats will soon arrive to make orb collection difficult, so just stay airborne and blast the Handguns in all directions.

When the lift reaches the top floor, jump to the higher level. The exit at the back will end the mission. Smash the crates and barrels in the area to release Red Orbs. Then check the door at the top of the steps on the left to find a Secret Room.

SECRET ROOM LOCATION 2

Trot up the stairs and examine the left door near the end of the mission to find a Secret Room.

MISSION COMPLETE!	
S RANK REQUIREMENTS	
CLEAR TIME	8:00 MINUTES
ORBS	4000
STYLISH AVERAGE	10 "SHOW TIME!!" COMBOS
DAMAGE	0
ITEM USED	NONE

MISSION 8

FURIATAURUS

RECOMMENDED SWORD	VENDETTA
RECOMMENDED GUN	SHOTGUN
RECOMMENDED AMULET	QUICK HEART, ELECTRO HEART, OFFENCE HEART

The slippery Arius summons quite a devil to cover his escape. Furiataurus charges its foe and knocks them to the ground, causing severe damage. Slamming the handle of its giant mace into the ground releases a powerful geyser of flame. The creature also spreads a circle of orange lights around it, all of which will soon burst into burning fire. Once it gets a big bonfire going, the creature whirls its mace in the air to create a powerful tornado that can draw in your hero from the farthest reaches of the oil platform. The last thing you want is to get hit by that big mace. The force alone is enough to reduce vitality by half and fling Dante through the air, and there's no telling how much damage the subsequent crash landing can cause. The Furiataurus also has a tendency to breathe fire in harder difficulty modes.

This giant flaming bull is strong versus flame and weak versus frost. Unfortunately, you don't have the correct Amulet Stone yet to inflict cold damage, but bear this vulnerability in mind for replay games. The Shotgun is the most damaging weapon, but only at Level 2 or 3. If you haven't had a chance to improve your boom stick yet, stick to the almighty Handguns. The same is true for the Vendetta.

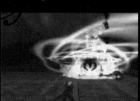

Distance is the safest bet. At the outset of the battle, run away! Head for one of the corners of the square oil derrick, where breakable objects might yield Green and Red Orbs. If Dante won't target the objects, then you'll just have to bait the Furiataurus into charging over and smashing the crates and barrels for you. Be sure to gather all the orbs from the outsides of the fighting zone, they provide your only chance of reaching the S rank requirements for this level.

When the Furiataurus charges, be sure to Air Hike ( ) far out of the way. The tornado attack, meant to draw Dante into a flame wreathe, can be resisted by Flip Escaping ⊙ away from the monster repeatedly.

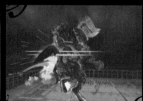

All the while you are retreating, baiting and dodging attacks, keep blasting away and filling those Devil Trigger gauges. Once Dante is ready to rip, be sure his Amulet is correctly loaded with the right stones and press [L1]. With the Quick Heart, you should be able to run behind Furiataurus easily. From its flank, attack swiftly and furiously with the sword. Watch the Devil Trigger gauges as you keep striking, and escape when you're almost out of juice. Return to the former strategy of retreating to the far corners of the platform and keep pumping the ⊙ button as fast as possible.

To get any Red Orbs from this monster, you must be standing directly beside the beast when its vitality bar empties. Also, you'll need to be at the "Show Time!!" level with a stylish combo in order to achieve the orbs requirement for the mission. Rejoice in the ease of this initial confrontation, because in harder difficulty modes the Furiataurus is so tricky it could very well stop your game!

MISSION COMPLETE!

S RANK REQUIREMENTS

CLEAR TIME	3:00 MINUTES
ORBS	1600
STYLISH AVERAGE	6 "SHOW TIME!!" COMBOS
DAMAGE	0
ITEM USED	NONE

MISSION 9

"Evil's course is plotted, and the dark disciple shall discard all that which he has built. Bursting and burning, the power source of the dark wizard will consume itself in hatred in only a short time. The hunter will discover the purity of speed."

-Guidepost for the Hunters *Chapter 8 Clause 2*

RUN FOR YOUR LIFE!

Upon reentering the building from the oil derrick platform, Dante will have only 12 minutes to race back through the underground train tunnel and the power plant. Dante must create an exit in the hangar just west of the entrance and leave the power plant before that time, or the devil hunter dies and even a Gold Orb won't save him!

FLAMING FIRE MONKEYS

Drop through the exact center of the elevator shaft, in order to collect a string of Red Orbs on the way down. The train is gone, so Dante must hike down the long tunnel on foot. However, an infinite number of Homromsira will respawn over and over on the train platform. Use this opportunity to build up your stylish combo average, fill your Devil Trigger gauges, and collect several thousand Red Orbs. Keep an eye on the timer, however, and leave the scene when 8 or more minutes remain.

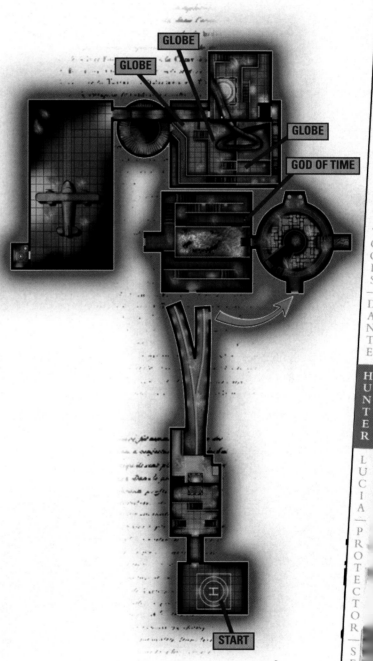

Much time can be wasted running down the train tunnel, so equip the Quick Heart and Devil Trigger. Scamper down the left tunnel to collect some Red Orbs, then back track a few steps and head down the right tunnel to the door. Release Dante from Devil Trigger and continue.

BEATING THE CLOCK

Run through the power cell room to the door on the opposite side. Red Orbs can be gained by jumping around both sides of the magma pit room, but only if you have the time. The God of Time statue is still functional if you want to level something up. Move quickly through the area, and ignore the Flambats as you work your way up the stairs to the exit.

The doors inside the silo are open, so if you have enough Devil Trigger power remaining in your gauges you can fly up through the middle of the cylindrical spiral staircase rather than run up all those stairs and face incidental enemy sets.

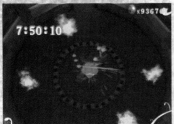 

Enter the silo center and strike the stone in the middle until it stops divulging Red Orbs. Equip the Aerial Heart in the Amulet and fly up through center, collecting more orbs from the platforms on either side. Fly through the top door on the left side, which is very close to the exit at the top of the stairs.

BACKYARD BRAWL

Three globe objects placed across the outdoor area must be struck and lit at the same time in order to unlock the shutter door at the top of the stairs. Jump to the left over the rail from the entrance, and quickly strike the first globe.

As you're heading toward the second globe on the next level up, a group of annoying Puia shall appear. This enemy set will never stop respawning, so you must ignore them and continue to strike the second and third globes. The only problem is that Dante's focus is drawn away from the globes to the enemies; making him strike the required objects becomes tricky. Position Dante near the globe and start shooting at the flying demons. While he's shooting, move Dante around the globe, and try to strike when you think he's facing the correct direction. This is easier than it sounds. When Dante has lit all three globes at the same time, the shutter door at the top will unlock. Quickly leap onto the stairs and exit. There's no time to lose!

Red Orbs line the tubes where Dante previously made a sliding entrance

Double-jump from the top stair, Devil Trigger and fly to the top of the spiraling tubes to find a **Blue Orb Fragment**.

HIGH WINDS IN THE HANGAR

Leap through the control room, and ignore the group of Terreofinis that appear. A large number of disc-throwing enemies will be included in this group, and you could very easily take some damage and lose your S ranking for the mission in this regard. Head for the high door on the other side of the room where a Red Orb sits.

Cross the corridor and enter the hangar, where a giant fan is sucking Dante toward the front of the room. Running against the draft, make your way across the room and enter the back of the cargo plane parked in the hangar. If time is lacking, use whatever Devil Trigger remains in your gauges in combination with the Quick Heart to make the trip more quickly.

Stepping inside the plane causes the aircraft to slide into the fan and destroy it. While inside the ship's hold, smash the large crate on the right side to obtain the **Missile Launcher**.

Exit the plane and run along the right side of the wreckage. Jump onto the lip of the demolished fan device, and enter the gaping hole made in the wall by the crash.

MISSION COMPLETE!	
S RANK REQUIREMENTS	
CLEAR TIME	6:00 MINUTES
ORBS	2000
STYLISH AVERAGE	20 "SHOW TIME!!" COMBOS
DAMAGE	0
ITEM USED	NONE

MISSION 10

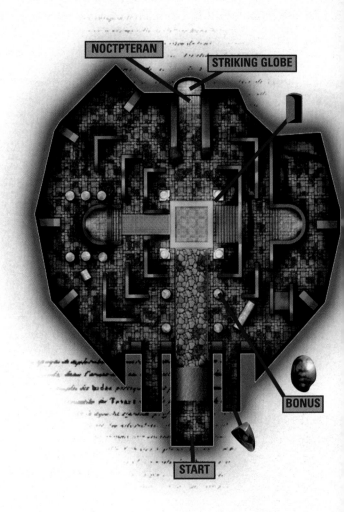

TEMPLE ENTRANCE

On either side of the arch covering the entrance point, there are two arches where Red Orbs wait to be collected. At the back of the archway to the right is a **Blue Orb Fragment**.

Jump on top of the broken pillar to the right of the tomb entrance, and move around the surface carefully until a cloud of **Bonus Red Orbs** falls from the sky!

Run around the outer edge of the circular area and collect the large Red Orbs tucked behind the parapets and support walls that surround the entire region. Pyromancers and their nasty brethren Auromancers may be encountered along the way. Build up your Devil Trigger gauge by blasting reappearing foes, until at least the first or second line is reached. Only then will Dante be able to open the door to the Tomb of Argosax, wherein the final Arcana item is protected.

AUROMANCER

Although no tougher in stamina or self-defense than Pyromancers, these hooded wizards cast a spell which fires icy homing missiles at Dante. For this reason alone, they provide a greater threat to the devil hunter than their flame-throwing siblings.

OPEN THE GATES

Once Dante's Devil Trigger gauges are at least quarter full, equip the Quick Heart in the Amulet and move to the globe object on either side of the area. Strike the object, then Devil Trigger and run straight across the center of the area toward the globe on the opposite side. Ignore the Auromancers that might appear, jump over the crumbled wall, reach the other globe and strike it before the first globe stops spinning. Only when both globes are struck in such a short amount of time will gates at the top of the area open.

SECRET ROOM LOCATION 1

After opening the gates, and before striking the globe object within, check the base of the tall column standing above and to the right of the temple entrance in the center of the area. Refer to the screenshot and the map to find the proper location.

GUARDIAN OF THE GATES

Enter the small alcove behind the opened gates, and strike the globe object until all purple squares are turned white. The stone doors covering the pit entrance to the temple slide back. But when you attempt to exit the alcove, a vortex forms under Dante and pulls him into an alternate dimension!

Defeat two Savage Golems and several bizarre flying creatures called Demonochorus. The enemy set will disappear when the two lumbering brutes are defeated, whether you have slain the Demonochorus or not. When the enemies are done for, the true monarch of this tiny domain arrives to test Dante's mettle.

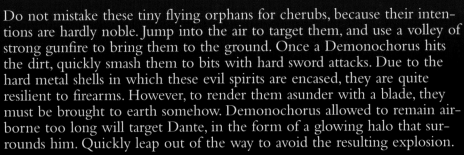

DEMONOCHORUS

Do not mistake these tiny flying orphans for cherubs, because their intentions are hardly noble. Jump into the air to target them, and use a volley of strong gunfire to bring them to the ground. Once a Demonochorus hits the dirt, quickly smash them to bits with hard sword attacks. Due to the hard metal shells in which these evil spirits are encased, they are quite resilient to firearms. However, to render them asunder with a blade, they must be brought to earth somehow. Demonochorus allowed to remain airborne too long will target Dante, in the form of a glowing halo that surrounds him. Quickly leap out of the way to avoid the resulting explosion.

NOCTPTERAN, LARVA

RECOMMENDED SWORD	REBELLION
RECOMMENDED GUN	SHOTGUN
RECOMMENDED AMULET	AERIAL HEART, FLAME HEART, OFFENCE HEART

The flying moth demon's main threat is that it will give birth to an endless supply of Larva. Therefore, it must be eliminated first. Air Hike (⊗ ⊗) high in the air directly beneath it. When Dante targets Noctpteran, hold R1 to lock on, and don't let go until the winged demon is permanently grounded. Do not remain on the ground more than an instant, or a Larva might attack Dante. Jump up and blast the massive monster with the shotgun, until the Devil Trigger gauges are full. With the Aerial Heart equipped, fly up to the Noctpteran's level, and blast it with rapid-fire flame attacks until the creature falls to the ground.

Although the Noctpteran is done for, it will eject several more Larva from its tail section before evaporating. Run to the rear side of the monster, equip the Missile Launcher and blast the newborn before they can escape into the earth. If you can prevent a few of these from burrowing, then there will be less to deal with for the rest of the battle.

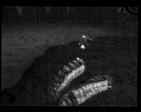

Full-grown Larva will erupt through the surface and chase after Dante. The surface is a dangerous place, especially while two or more Larvae are still active. Every time Dante lands, jump immediately. If it looks like he's about to fall directly into a Larva's mouth, press ⊗ again to Air Hike away. Use the Shotgun to blast their hides, and make wise use of the Green Orbs at the four corners of the area.

If a Larva swallows Dante, rapidly wiggle the Left Analog Stick and roll your thumb over the face buttons of the controller to get free. Although Dante takes severe damage, he frees himself from the Larva by ripping it in half! This is also a valid way to defeat the Larva and end the battle, but at some cost of vitality.

When only one Larva remains, wait for it to surface and remain still for a moment. Devil Trigger and fly over the carrion crawler, filling it with underworld-powered bullets. Following the death of the last Larva, a portal to the normal world shall appear.

DOWN YOU GO!

Returning to the temple entrance, all that remains to complete the mission is to drop through the square opening in the center of the area.

MISSION COMPLETE!	
S RANK REQUIREMENTS	
CLEAR TIME	5:00 MINUTES
ORBS	3500
STYLISH AVERAGE	10 "SHOW TIME!!" COMBOS
DAMAGE	0
ITEM USED	NONE

MISSION 11

"The hunter must plummet to great depths within the earth, and leap to great heights. The machinations of the Old World must be discovered anew. For the underground temple of Argosax is guarded by his most skilled warrior. He wields a spear and is obeyed by the wolves. His single eye possesses knowledge and hate. He is the one who brings misfortune."

-Guidepost for the Hunters *Chapter 9 Clause 6*

SIDE VIEW MAPS

The maps for this mission are side view, as opposed to the top-down maps in the rest of Dante's game.

START

BONUS

STRIKING STONE

STRIKING GLOBE

TOMB ENTRANCE

Proceed down the ramp and check the short wall bearing the "eye" design to find a Secret Room. On a brightly colored landing further down, Dante must dismantle some easy Agonofinis and Goatling enemies. Continue down the suspended ledges until Dante enters a door.

Two breakable sarcophagi stand in a niche below the entrance platform.

Sealed behind a large door, move to either side of the platform and drop over the edge. Defeat a set of poisonous Gbusmsira and smash all the sarcophagi in the room for Red Orbs.

SECRET ROOM LOCATION 1

Descending along the ramp from the starting point, examine the eye design at the second corner you come to on the path to find a Secret Room.

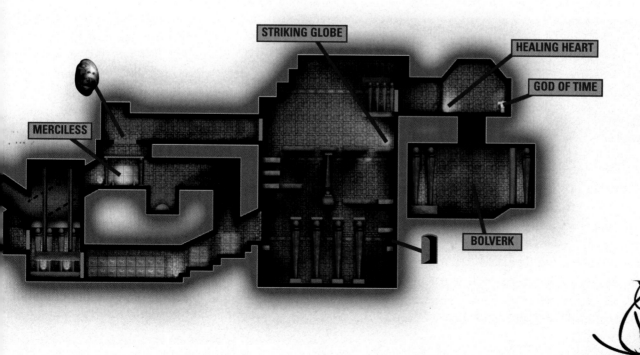

STRIKING GLOBE

HEALING HEART

GOD OF TIME

MERCILESS

BOLVERK

GBUSMSIRA

These monsters are a stronger variation of Msira, with higher levels of vitality. Their veins are filled with venom, and they can spit a substance that inflicts poison status for several moments. Their regular attacks, such as claw swipes and tackles, can cause poisoning as well. Keep your distance from them while shooting, and strike with the sword to spark stylish combos only when they are off-balance or staggering.

ROTATION CHAMBER

Proceed up the corridor and drop through an opening onto a ledge in a large round room. Move to the left, collecting Red Orbs floating in front of little red doorways situated around the top of the room.

Jump into the high alcove two spaces down and to the left of the entrance to find **Bonus Red Orbs**!

Strike the globe on the central pedestal to rotate the room. The entrance platform now rests against the opposite wall, and you may continue into the tomb. Fend off the cluster of Demonochorus, which arrive, and build up your Devil Trigger gauges for the task just ahead. Leap through the large opening and continue up the corridor.

BOULDER DASH!

Smash the two sarcophagi at the top of a winding ramp to obtain a **Green Orb** and a Red Orb. Slash away at the striking stone in the square area to release as many orbs as you can before time runs out. Equip the Quick Heart in the Amulet, to prepare for a maddening chase.

When Dante steps into the sloping corridor just past the striking stone, a magic ball falls from the ceiling and starts to roll after him. If the rolling ball strikes Dante, he will be

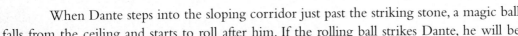

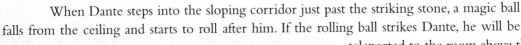

teleported to the room above the striking stone and must defeat two Savage Golems in a very tight space before he will be released. In order to outrun the ball and drop into the next room, Dante must Devil Trigger and run like the wind using the Quick Heart. If your DT gauges are dry, you'll just have to keep killing Savage Golems until you're ready to make the dash.

SPIKE SLAM

The chamber that Dante drops into houses an evil trap. A large metal slab raises and drops, crushing anything beneath it. Blocking the exit on the other side is a large square stone with a chaos symbol painted upon it. Wait until the spiky slab rises and start to run underneath as it ascends. Smash the square stone a few times with Vendetta, and keep an eye on the spiky slab. As the spiked platform almost reaches the top, run to the safe area on the left side of the screen. It's better to retreat too soon than risk a few extra attacks on the stone square, just to get crushed under the spikes. Dante suffers major damage if caught under the metal trap.

SECRET CHAMBER OF THE MERCILESS

When the painted square stone is finally smashed out of the way, a secret doorway in the back wall on the left side of the screen opens. A low Kick Jump will deliver Dante into this hidden corridor.

Run up the ramp into a room where Dante can acquire two Red Orbs and the sword **Merciless**. This is the perfect weapon to use against all types of Msira, as well as spell-casting wizards.

Inside the room, move toward the camera and stop when you can see an area overhead. Jump through the narrow slit up to a domed area with four Red Orbs and an entire **Blue Orb**!

When you jump off the ledge from the secret room, Dante lands in the corridor just beyond the spike trap room. Retreat a few steps to smash two stone sarcophagi holding large Red Orbs. Then proceed up the stairs into another gigantic puzzle area.

THE PLATFORM ROOM

Drop to the lower floor, and head around the outside of the room to the left. Jump onto a small platform on the left wall to release a swarm of **Bonus Red Orbs**.

Continue around the outside of the square room until Dante comes under a trio of platforms. Use one of the two lower small platforms to hop up to the wider

platform above. Search the archway against the wall on this platform to discover a Secret Room. Continue to the next platform, and jump across a series of magic platforms suspended in space high over the floor.

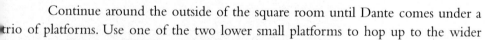

AERIAL HEART SHORTCUT

When Dante is in a position to jump across the suspended squares, there are some columns supporting a platform on the level overhead. Kick Jump off the wall, Devil Trigger in mid air and fly onto the higher platform. This allows you to skip an entire level of tricky jumps! Plus, you can glide right over to the exit, without having to engage the central lift platform in the chamber.

GUIDE | MASTERY | DEMONIC | POWER | DEVILISH | TOOLS | DANTE | HUNTER | LUCIA | PROTECTOR | SECRETS

MISSION

11

HIDDEN ALCOVES AND WINKING PLATFORMS

Jump around the room, until Dante arrives in a corner where the platform overhead fades in and out of existence. Use this disappearing platform to reach a small passageway high in the wall. Smash the two sarcophagi in this corridor for large Red Orbs, and then continue to the end to obtain the **Submachine Guns**! Although these dual semi-automatics saturate their targets with lead, they have considerable less firepower than your other guns. Still, these are the best guns to use against foes that yield no orbs, such as Flambats and certain bosses.

CEILING LEVEL

Proceed to jump across the disappearing platforms, leaping before each level disappears from under Dante's feet. The path leads Dante to a key object globe on a platform against the wall. When all purple squares surrounding the globe have

been bashed white, a square lift in the center of the room becomes activated. Drop down to the ground level, and stand in the center of the square. Dante is raised to the ceiling level. Hop off at your stop, and proceed through the corridor.

BASH FOR THE GEM

Destroy two sarcophagi in the corridor for Red Orbs, and proceed into a small square chamber where three more ancient coffins stand in a row. These sarcophagi are especially hard to smash, and they will reappear in just a few seconds after being smashed. An Amulet Stone is located in the next chamber, and it is encased in a protective shield. The shield only deactivates when the three sarcophagi are smashed. You must smash all three stone coffins and dash into the next room before any of the sarcophagi reappear, in order to obtain the Amulet Stone.

Equip the Quick Heart to be prepared for this challenge, and use a Devil Star S. if your gauges are empty.

Each standing coffin requires at least 24 hits to smash, even if you're in Devil Trigger mode. Start by attacking the sarcophagus on the left, and deliver roughly 22 whacks to it. Then move Dante between the second two sarcophagi, and attack the middle one 22 times. Finally, move to the outside of the line and attack the third sarcophagus until it breaks. Now you should be able to smash the second two objects easily. The one you attacked first will have regenerated a few structural points, so it will probably take 6 to 8 chops to destroy. Before any of the stone coffins reappear, Devil Trigger and dash into the next chamber before the blue force field reappears around the gem.

With the **Healing Heart** equipped in the Amulet, Dante regenerates vitality while he is in Devil Trigger. This will be especially important against the next incredibly tough boss!

Use the God of Time statue to improve the Merciless, then drop through the hole in the floor.

64

BOLVERK, FREKI & GERI

RECOMMENDED SWORD	VENDETTA
RECOMMENDED GUN	HANDGUNS
RECOMMENDED AMULET	QUICK HEART, FLAME HEART, HEALING HEART

Standing in the center of this area is suicidal while Bolverk and his two mascots are zipping back and forth as fast as they please. Retreat to one corner of the room (preferably onto the raised area to either side of the large exit door). Pound the two dogs with bullets, and work to raise the Devil Trigger gauges.

Once you've baited the two wolves and their master into the corner, Devil Trigger and slash away at all three of them. Hopefully this will be sufficient to take out one if not both of the phantom hounds, so that only the demon knight remains to be dealt with.

Bolverk is a tough and swift foe, but he can still be defeated. Any attempt to shoot him from afar results in suffering from the dark one's ranged attacks. Although tricky, the best method is to take Bolverk head on with Dante's strongest sword attacks. It's possible to cause the boss to stagger, if enough sword blows can be struck in a row. As soon as your power gauges reach the first line, use Devil Trigger immediately to reduce Bolverk's vitality by another yard. Keep slashing away in this manner, using Devil Trigger in short bursts to alleviate the tremendous advantage this boss has over Dante.

MISSION COMPLETE!

S RANK REQUIREMENTS

CLEAR TIME	8:30 MINUTES
ORBS	4500
STYLISH AVERAGE	6 "SHOW TIME!!" COMBOS
DAMAGE	0
ITEM USED	NONE

MISSION 12

"It is a sphere of death, a rotating electric field which feeds power to the whole. The hunter must smash the ancient machinery to open the path to the protector. When the hunter and protector meet, the last mystery will be revealed. But the hunter must attend to what the Protector left behind."

-Guidepost for the Hunters *Chapter 9 Clause 9*

SECRET ROOM LOCATION 1

Immediately after starting the mission, check the large double doors behind Dante, engraved with the fresco.

ELECTRIC NIGHTMARE

Proceed into a spherical chamber to start an extremely dangerous combat event. A decorative globe in the center of the chamber emits an electrical field, stretched between eight diamond-shaped transmitters. The electric field is only dangerous at the edges, so Dante remains safe as long as he is close to directly under the central globe.

While trying to remain directly under the central globe, Air Hike into the air and press ⓨ with the right timing to strike one of the eight transmitters. Only one direct hit is required to smash each one. When all eight are destroyed, the spherical room stops spinning and the exit is revealed. The only hitch is that four Sargassos are positioned around center sphere, and they will not only attack Dante, but also draw his aim away from the diamond objects.

Double-jump high into the air and press ⓨ at the height of the leap in order to smash whatever is above. If all four of the Sargasso skulls are destroyed, they will all respawn immediately. Make your life easier by smashing three of the Sargassos, and stay on the opposite side of the center globe from the remaining skull. As the number of diamond transmitter objects decrease, time your jumps to hit the last few remainders.

SARGASSO

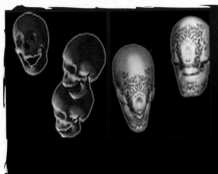

Phantom skulls from the demon world, these avatars of doom are posted to stand vigilant in key locations so that the other demons may roam and prey. Sargassos appear in two varieties: the more regular skull-shaped type and also the brightly painted large kind. Sargassos remain spectral and cannot be damaged until your character is in extremely close proximity to them. Once they materialize, they will swoop in to attack quite swiftly. The best strategy is to move close to them, then jump away and pulverize them with the Shotgun.

CORRIDOR TO DESTINY

When the electric field is dismantled and the room stops rolling, drop through the pit in the center of the room. Replenish vitality with a **Green Orb** at one end of the room, and use the God of Time statue on the opposite wall.

In the first alcove on the left side, jump inside the alcove to discover a bevy of **Bonus Red Orbs**.

Proceed into the short corridor and smash the sarcophagi standing in the alcoves on the left and right. As you get close to the door at the end of the corridor, be extremely careful not to go through the door before smashing the standing coffins to the left and right, and reaping their bittersweet rewards.

SECRET ROOM LOCATION 2

Smash the stone sarcophagus to the left of the exit from the corridor, step into the alcove and search to find a Secret Room.

PLUTONIAN

RECOMMENDED SWORD	VENDETTA
RECOMMENDED GUN	HANDGUNS
RECOMMENDED AMULET	QUICK HEART, ELECTRO HEART, HEALING HEART

After a brief reunion with Lucia, it looks like the devil hunter has to finish what the protector started. Plutonian is a prisoner of the demon world, but his chains can hardly contain him. Instead, he whips around the two massive iron balls at the ends of his restraints and uses them as weapons to pulverize Dante.

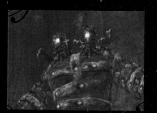

Fire bullets at Plutonian from a distance in order to raise your Devil Trigger gauges. Stay out of range of the iron balls, and use Air Hike (⊗ ⊗) or Flip Escape ⊙ to avoid his long throws. When the Devil Trigger gauges have filled, shoot at Plutonian until he begins to deflect bullets by swinging one of his chains in a circle. Devil Trigger and dash quickly behind the oversized monster. Attack him from the rear with electrically charged sword attacks. Keep an eye on your Devil Trigger gauge as you strike, and leap away following the instant Dante returns to his normal state. Retreat and recharge the Devil Trigger gauge by attacking from a distance.

This strategy is easy enough for someone with Dante's skills to follow, but the situation is complicated when laser beams fire across the room. Take warning of the damaging rays when a faint blue beam of light begins to grow brighter. Jump or Flip Escape out of the path of the beam. Since the beams start at one side of the room and progress to the other, you should escape in the direction where the beams have already been. After the beams fire across the wide of the room, they will begin to fire across the length of the room in the same one by one fashion. But before long, both sets of beams will be firing simultaneously creating a net of lasers across the ground. When the lasers start to form in a grid, Air Hike high in the room and keep Dante aloft by firing the Handguns rapidly.

Terreofinis soldiers will appear in the battle zone, and move to attack. Use strong sword attacks against these creatures to rebuild the power in your Devil Trigger gauges quickly, so that you can approach and attack Plutonian once more. If too many Terreofinis converge on Dante, try to stay in one area until the big brute throws his iron ball and smashes all the caged skeletons out of the way like toys!

Once Plutonian has fallen for the last time, collect the Red Orbs he leaves behind and board the elevator back up to the surface. Mission complete!

MISSION COMPLETE!	
S RANK REQUIREMENTS	
CLEAR TIME	6:30 MINUTES
ORBS	3500
STYLISH AVERAGE	8 "SHOW TIME!!" COMBOS
DAMAGE	0
ITEM USED	NONE

MISSION 13

"Bidden by the summoner, the hunter flips the coin of destiny to determine the fate of the protector. Evil keeps her hostage in the tower of corruption. The hunter will learn to feel with a leap of faith."

-Guidepost for the Hunters *Chapter 10 Clause 3*

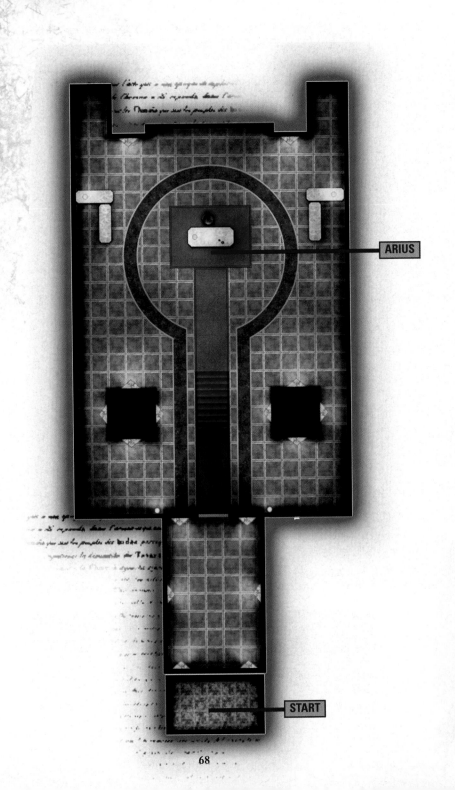

ARIUS

START

ARIUS

RECOMMENDED SWORD	MERCILESS
RECOMMENDED GUN	SHOTGUN
RECOMMENDED AMULET	QUICK HEART, FLAME HEART, HEALING HEART

Oddly, the genius mastermind behind Auroboros and the whole evil scheme isn't much of a tough guy. Arius attacks only with a pistol, and various dark spells such as Black Hole and Shadow Spike. He can make himself invulnerable for brief periods merely by erecting a protective shell around himself, but it doesn't last long. The main complication in this battle is the monsters Arius might summon to attack Dante. As the battle progresses, the evil sorcerer will conjure tougher creatures such as Blood Goats, and then things might get ugly. The key is to try to ignore the Jomothumsira, which crouch at the master's feet, and target Arius himself for all of your attacks.

Use the Shotgun to blast Jomothumsiras out of the way. Slash Arius with the sword Merciless, and build your Devil Trigger gauges. If Arius teleports to a side of the room and sits idly on a desk, avoid battling any of the minor monsters and dash after the dark wizard, using Devil Trigger and the Quick Heart to move with blinding speed. Keep slashing away at Arius with strong sword attacks and Devil Trigger whenever the first line of your gauges is reached. It's pretty amusing to be able to fling Arius up in the air or over a desk, try it sometime!

JOMOTHUMSIRA

The toughest form of monkey-like demons, Jomothumsiras are almost impossible to knock off balance until their vitality is low, and their attacks are strong enough to knock even Dante off his feet! Use Shotgun blasts to keep them at bay, and try to eliminate groups with the Missile Launcher. Jomothumsiras are prime candidates to try the entire High Time move, with an uppercut, two mid-air kicks, followed by a hard chop to the ground. Tough monkeys deserve tough punishment!

MISSION COMPLETE!

S RANK REQUIREMENTS	
CLEAR TIME	2:30 MINUTES
ORBS	2500
STYLISH AVERAGE	6 "SHOW TIME!!" COMBOS
DAMAGE	0
ITEM USED	NONE

MISSION 14

"The power of the demon world can warp the minds of men and stop the hands of time. In the time between seconds, reality is not what it seems. The dark forces can bend passages that once led to real destinations into circles of infinite confusion. The hunter must seek out and activate the keyposts of the demon realm. Four lights will open the door to the future and the past."

-Guidepost for the Hunters *Chapter 11 Clause 7*

WARPED BY THE ECLIPSE

Things have gotten extremely weird in the southern township of Vidu Mali. The city no longer extends from the southern tip to the middle of the island. The entire town has been warped by the approach of the demon world into a viscous infinite circle, and what was once recognizable now connects together in ways you'd have never thought possible. To open the gateway out of this bizarre realm, you must locate four globes and strike them until a ring forms around each. Only then will you be able to open the portal.

At the start of the mission, head toward the God of Time statue behind Dante. Check the doors to the left, which used to be the trolley station entrance, to find a Secret Room. Proceed up the street and through a broken doorway to a familiar but twisted area.

SECRET ROOM LOCATION 1

Check the door that used to lead to the old trolley station, and you'll find the next Secret Room.

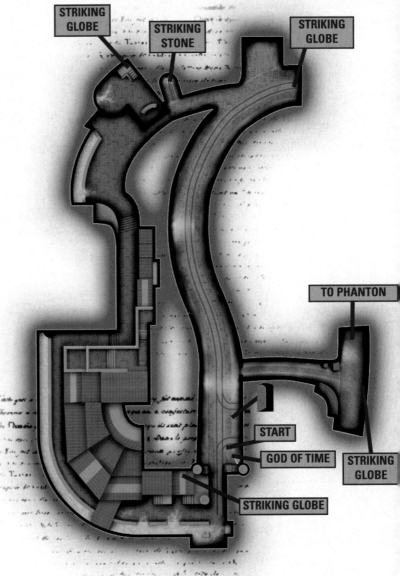

70

THE FIRST GLOBE

Proceed past the buildings and take on an extremely tough group of Abyss Goats, which are the top dogs in the goat demon brood. These floating monstrosities aren't difficult to take on one by one. But when three of them appear (such as in this situation), you'll need the Missile Launcher to bring them down! Perform a Flip Escape between each rocket shot, just to stay out of the path of the homing projectiles they fire.

Try to jump on top of the tilting column on the right corner, to release a bevy of **Bonus Red Orbs**!

Move toward the low wall blocking the street, and jump onto the rooftops to the right. Kick Jump up the side of the building to the incredibly high roof. Run to the right until Dante finds a large Red Orb and a globe suspended high in the air. How in the world are you going to hit that thing, way up there?

ABYSS GOAT

Kings among the goat-headed demons, the Abyss Goats are larger than the rest and have the sturdiest wings. Abyss Goats won't hesitate to take to the air and cast a deluge of magic missiles to track a target. A constant barrage of gunfire will eventually cause them to convulse in mid air, but they can remain aloft even after such an attack! Disrupt their aerial attacks by blasting them with the Missile Launcher. If an Abyss Goat does fall to the ground, chop them up really well using the Vendetta.

STRIKING A HIGH GLOBE

Button mashing is counter-productive in activating a globe placed really high. Position Dante directly under the globe and Air Hike with two hard and well timed presses on the ✕ button. When Dante rises just above the level of the globe, press △ to chop it with your sword. As Dante lands, he needs a split second to recover. Watch his animation carefully. As soon as he is upright, press ✕ twice again to begin your next Air Hike. If you press ✕ too soon, you might mess up and not be able to make the second jump. It's important to strike the globe again before the little square you turned purple reverts to white, otherwise you'll be losing ground in the battle to strike that globe! Repeat as swiftly as possible until the globe is encircled and the demon world draws nearer.

HARD ENEMY SET!

In a corner formed by the rooftops are several Red Orbs to collect. Crossing the low wall that divides the street triggers one of the most enormous and dangerous enemy sets in the game. Abyss Goats join with Blood Goats to flood the sky with magic missiles that hone in on Dante, while disc-whipping Agonofinis make the street a very dangerous place to stand. Remain on the rooftops and use the Missile Launcher or Shotgun to take the flying goat demons out of the skies. Then drop to the ground and smash all the cage skeletons. Retreat to the safety of the rooftops when the enemy set respawns a second time.

The trick is to manage killing all the flying goats in spite of strange camera angles on the rooftops.

REVENGE OF THE MONKEYS

At the end of the long street, jump onto the lowest balcony to obtain a Red Orb. Proceed along the street and take out a large group of Jomothumsira and Gbusmsira, using the Submachine Guns to keep Dante safe from poison attacks.

Proceed down the steps and along the street, and pick up a Red Orb in the corner. Continue to the right and jump through the high archway into the same courtyard where you met the original Msira. This time, you must defeat a large group of Jomothumsira teamed up with Brontomancers, who will cast lightning spells unless Dante eliminates them quickly. With the evil wizards out of the picture, Dante can easily strike some stylish combos off the shadow monkeys.

BRONTOMANCER

Appearing and disappearing to avoid harm, these spell-casting wizards are no stronger than their relatives but certainly are cleverer. Brontomancers cast lightning spells, which strike almost without warning, so whenever you see one of these enemies conjuring it's time to slash them into next week. Brontomancers attack and evade at higher rates than other dark spell casters.

GLOBE NUMBER TWO

On a small plat-form in the corner, strike the globe until a ring surrounds it. Just two more to go, and the gateway shall open.

EVERYTHING YOU MISSED

If Dante failed to find the Merciless in a previous mission, it will be standing in the corner near the sphere that must be struck. Also, if you didn't have the patience to get the Healing Heart by smashing the coffins near Bolverk's lair, a small altar will be against the wall nearby. Defeat all the enemies in the courtyard to finally get the stone. This is a much easier way to obtain it!

DEAD END GLOBE

Jump out of the courtyard and follow a string of little Red Orbs into the next area. Divert briefly into the right niche, and slash at a striking stone to get all the orbs you can in just a few seconds.

Proceed forward from the Y-shaped intersection to the dead end of the street. Defeat a group of Savage Golems and Demonochorus, then strike the globe near the large wooden gate until it is ringed in blue. Return to the Y-intersection and head down the street to the left.

Equip the Aerial Heart, Devil Trigger and fly up to the top of the side area near the third globe to find a **Gold Orb** floating midair.

THE WIZARDS' HAUNT

Defeat or ignore a set of disc-spinning Agonofinis, and continue down the street. Leap up to grab tiny Red Orbs suspended high on the tilted wall, and keep moving down the slope until you arrive at the starting point of the mission. A large Red Orb highlights a side corridor branching off to the left.

Run down the narrow alley until you spot a Red Orb on top of a familiar ledge. The **Blue Orb Fragment** on the next ledge higher up is too far away to reach by jumping. Equip the Aerial Heart in the Amulet, then Air Hike high up into the air. Devil Trigger midair, and glide to a position above the ledge. Dante will slowly sink down onto the ledge and grab the fragment.

You will probably not reach the Blue Orb Fragment without triggering the appearance of a massive group of wizards. Pyromancers, Auromancers and Brontomancers ambush Dante and cast spells from all sides! Retreat back into the narrow alley. The more confined zone makes it harder for the spell casters to surround the devil hunter, and easier to dispatch them.

When the coast is clear, perform Air Hikes to reach the globe suspended in midair, and strike it until it activates. If you're having trouble, refer to the previous description of *"Striking a High Globe"*, just a few pages back. Head through the tall door to the left.

GATEWAY TO THE PAST

To reach the future, one must be willing to open the door to the past. Having activated all four globes in the level, the eyeballs surrounding the gateway in the center of this area should be hatched. A single eye emerges from the central core. Move to the eyeball and strike it to encounter an old adversary once again.

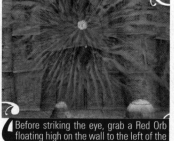

Before striking the eye, grab a Red Orb floating high on the wall to the left of the entrance.

If Dante lacks in health, a **Green Orb** hovers high on the wall to the right of the entrance. Leave it for the boss fight if you don't need it.

PHANTOM

RECOMMENDED SWORD	VENDETTA
RECOMMENDED GUN	SUBMACHINE GUNS OR HANDGUNS
RECOMMENDED AMULET	QUICK HEART, ELECTRO HEART, OFFENCE HEART

Ah yes, a fond trip down memory lane. Or not. After its dismal failures in the previous game, the Phantom has been granted yet another chance by the forces of darkness and time paradox to challenge the Son of Sparda yet again. You just can't keep a good magma spider down!

Encased entirely in stony sediment, the only weakness of the Phantom is its head. In the initial stages of the battle run at the Phantom, jump onto its back like the cocky devil hunter you are, and pump those guns rapid-fire. The overgrown bug will attempt to buck off Dante, so if you're tossed from the beast you can just jump right back on. Keep pumping bullets into the monster's head with either the Submachine Guns or Handguns, whichever is higher in level. Eventually the rear section of the Phantom will uncurl into a deadly scorpion-style tail, and your merry ride must end. Do not attempt to jump onto the Phantom's back once his tail is out, because the sting is worse than ever!

For the rest of the battle, leap high over the Phantom and blast it from above. Keep using your arsenal weapons until Dante's Devil Trigger gauges are ready to go. Then land on the ground, run at the Phantom's head and Devil Trigger. Then slash away at the spider's exposed skull, but keep a firm eye on your DT gauges. When Dante's superpower runs out, leap away as fast as possible. The Phantom has a devastating new attack where it seizes the Devil Hunter, squeezes some life out of him, and then bashes him to the ground for good measure. This big freak isn't messing around this time!

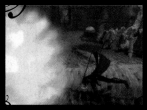

If the Phantom becomes very still, even when Dante is attacking at close range, it's time to start rolling. The Phantom can cause geysers of lava to shoot up from the ground, preceded only by a little ruffle of dust on the ground. Use Flip Escape ⊙ to avoid magma columns, and don't worry about attacking until the Phantom ceases this attack. The same is true for when the extended tail fires a meteor into the sky. Small but devastating meteorites will pelt the ground for several moments after this, but they can be avoided in the same fashion if you focus on dodging for a few seconds, rather than attack.

The Phantom becomes harder and harder as you progress through the increasing difficulty levels. Enjoy your victory now while it lasts, because the big spider bully may have the final laugh later on!

MISSION COMPLETE!	
S RANK REQUIREMENTS	
CLEAR TIME	7:30 MINUTES
ORBS	6500
STYLISH AVERAGE	15 "SHOW TIME!!" COMBOS
DAMAGE	0
ITEM USED	NONE

MISSION 15

"Opening a passage through the demon world summons the denizens of the dark to protect the gateway. They swarm like clouds and desperately seek the hunter's dark blood. All must be laid waste before the gate can be entered unprotected."

-Guidepost for the Hunters *Chapter 11 Clause 9*

ONSLAUGHT

Strike the central eye again, in another attempt to wrench open the demon gate. A timer appears onscreen, and enemies quickly surround Dante. The idea is to defeat a powerful double enemy set in less than three minutes. The first wave includes Jomothumsira and Demonochorus. The second wave consists mainly of Abyss Goats. The winged goat demons will quickly gang up on Dante if you move around too much, so try to stay on one side of the circular area. Let them come to you, and use flame attacks in Devil Trigger to bash away the Abyss Goats.

If you fail to defeat all the enemies before three minutes expires, the gate closes and the fighting stops. You've also lost your chance at an S ranking. Strike the central eye again to try and open the gate again. This time you'll face a much easier enemy set, and four minutes to defeat them.

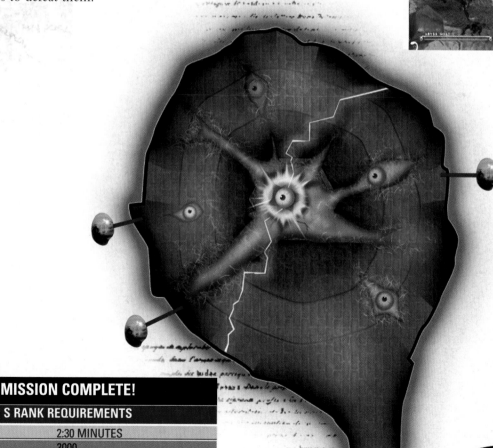

MISSION COMPLETE!	
S RANK REQUIREMENTS	
CLEAR TIME	2:30 MINUTES
ORBS	3000
STYLISH AVERAGE	10 "SHOW TIME!!" COMBOS
DAMAGE	0
ITEM USED	NONE

MISSION 16

"Chaos ripens as the hunter runs toward the sky. When the hungry mouth is fed, the body is subjected to changes. Only through inviting the change and coming closer to the demon world will the hunter find the path through the intestines of evil. Rising from the bowels, the hunter must confront the head."

-Guidepost for the Hunters *Chapter 12 Clause 1*

MAP OF METAMORPHOSIS

Each time a Sacrilege is fed to one of the hungry mouth doors, the entire layout of the level changes. The maps in this section change along with the game.

LOBBY SECURITY

Head toward the doors of the lobby to initial a battle with several Blood Goats. All of the Blood Goats must be defeated in order to unseal the lobby doors.

Head upstairs, and move Dante into the corner just above and to the left of the lobby doors to unleash **Bonus Red Orbs**.

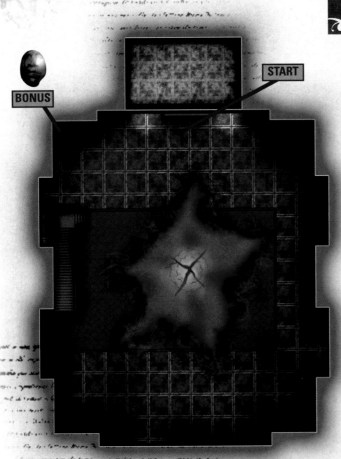

BONUS

START

76

TAKE THE STAIRS

Instead of getting cornered or surrounded by the herd, position Dante on the steps, where the big enemies don't have much room to maneuver and <u>they can be defeated one by one.</u>

WHAT FLOOR, PLEASE?

Equip a swift sword like Rebellion or Merciless, depending on which is higher in level. Enter the elevator and move to one of the lower corners. En route, a large group of Terreofinis and their higher brethren Mortfinis will invade the elevator car. If you can't score a full "Show Time!!" combo off an easy, tightly packed group like this, then obviously you haven't been playing the game!

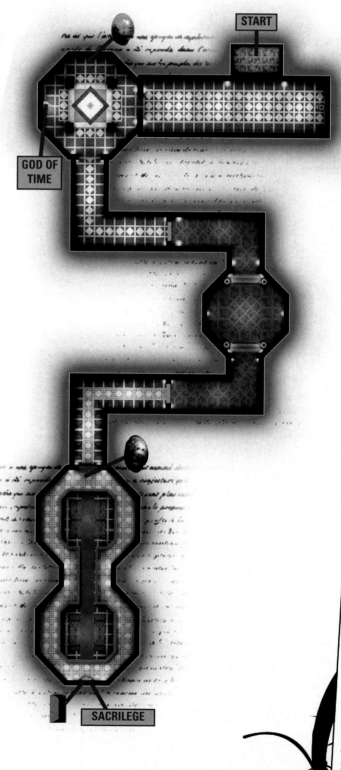

START

GOD OF TIME

SACRILEGE

MORTFINIS

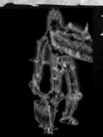

The last of the final form monsters, Mortfinis are slightly stronger in vitality and attack than Terreofinis and Agonofinis. If you've been leveling up your swords and weapons, they are still not a problem to deal with.

EXECUTIVE SUITES

Run left from the elevator doors and smash the vase at the end of the hall for Red Orbs. Do the same with the other vases and pots found throughout the level.

Proceed into the octagonal room at the end of the hallway, and use the God of Time statue if so inclined. This shop location will remain here if the floors should happen to shift a little. Smash the green vase to the left of the statue to get a **Green Orb**.

DODGE BALL

Continue into the connecting corridor and smash all the vases to obtain orbs. In the third section the floor, the door is engraved with a large ugly face. Inspection shows that the mouth is hungry for something.

Entering the double-octagonal main room, more of those glowing boulders begin shooting across the room. Getting hit by any of the translucent balls teleports Dante into an alternative realm where he must destroy two Savage Golems while braving the disc throwing of several Mortfinis.

Stick to the outside edges of the room. Try to Air Hike up to the balcony, where avoiding the boulders is much easier. The magic boulders will quit rolling when the area near the object glittering on the upper level is reached. Take the **Sacrilege** and return to the door.

On the upper balcony, near the entrance, is a whole **Blue Orb**!

SECRET ROOM LOCATION 1

Check the wall panel on the lower level of the double octagon room, right below the spot where you obtained the first Sacrilege. Dante enters a Secret Room.

REARRANGING CORRIDORS

When the Sacrilege is placed into the foul mouth, a great rumbling occurs. The connecting corridor that Dante reenters is quite unlike the one he visited before.

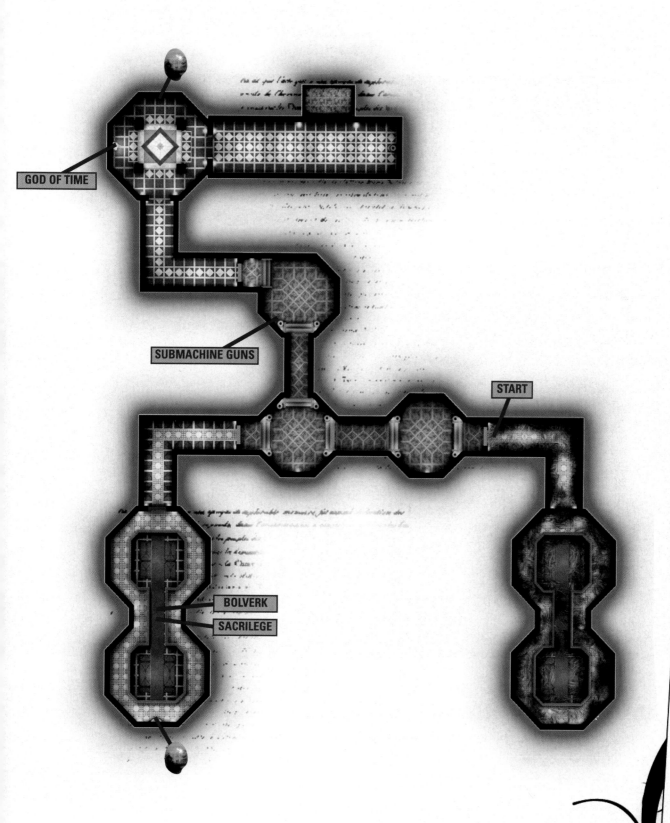

GOD OF TIME

SUBMACHINE GUNS

START

BOLVERK

SACRILEGE

TWO WAY GREEN

Smash all the new vases in the new connecting corridor, and defeat spell casters in each large area. Don't miss out on the orbs in the square area near the elevator corridor or the **Submachine Guns** hidden in one of the vases in the top-left octagonal room. Head to the new double-octagonal room on the east side of the level.

REAPPEARING GREEN ORBS

The vase to the right of the God of Time statue in the elevator corridor seems to respawn after the first change in corridor layout. Pretty handy, if you need another **Green Orb** to recover.

BOLVERK, FREKI & GERI

RECOMMENDED SWORD	VENDETTA
RECOMMENDED GUN	SUBMACHINE GUNS
RECOMMENDED AMULET	QUICK HEART, FLAME HEART, HEALING HEART

Guess who's back to settle his score with the Sparda family? Finding a corner in this twisted double octagonal room will be more difficult, so prepare to take a lot of hits from the twin white wolves until you manage to defeat them. As for Bolverk, keep a much closer eye on the demon knight and leap just as the skeletal lord is winding up to attack.

The wolves move much faster than their master does, so use that to your advantage. Lead Freki and Geri to the opposite end of the room, where a **Green Orb** sits if you need it. Pound away at one of the wolves until Bolverk obviously catches up to the three of you, then escape and lead the wolves to the other side of the room. Build up your Devil Trigger gauges by blasting and spearing the wolves.

When the white familiars collapse, fight Bolverk in much the same fashion as your previous experience. Flip Escape to avoid his attacks, then use hard sword attacks to knock him off balance if possible. Anytime your Devil Trigger gauge gets above one line, use it on the demon knight in a burst of fiery sword strikes. And whatever you do, watch out for the seal covering the doorway! This is the last you'll see of daddy's old nemesis. Good riddance!

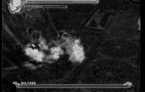

THE SECOND SACRILEGE

Bolverk collapses, leaving behind another **Sacrilege**. Return to the entrance of the room and insert it into the hungry door to change the appearance of the corridor outside once again.

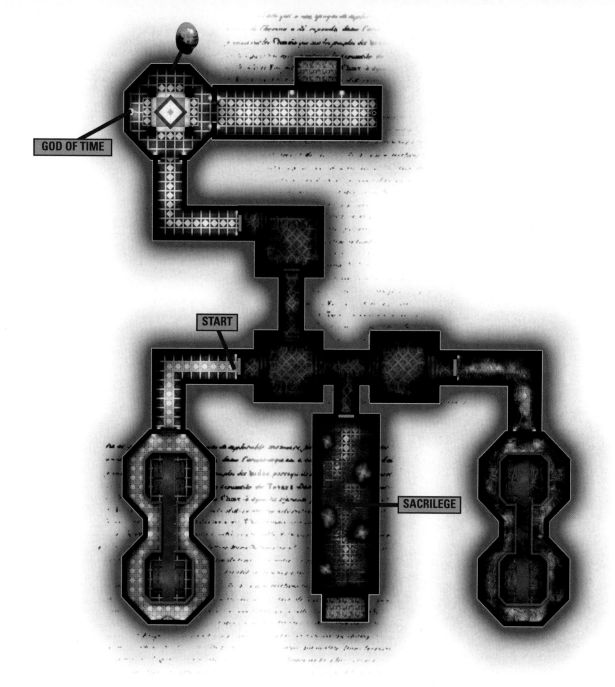

GOD OF TIME

START

SACRILEGE

DECAYING PASSAGE

Check your in-game map to see that a new room has appeared between the
two bottom double-octagonal rooms (or check out the map on this page). A string
of small Red Orbs leads you right to the door.

FINAL SACRILEGE

Defeat a good-sized set of Abyss Goats and Demonochorus in an extremely tiny s[...]
obtain the last **Sacrilege**. Although there is an elevator door at the bottom of this room,
enter the elevator. Instead, place the Sacrilege into the hungry door, to rearrange the level[...]
time.

ABYSS GOAT

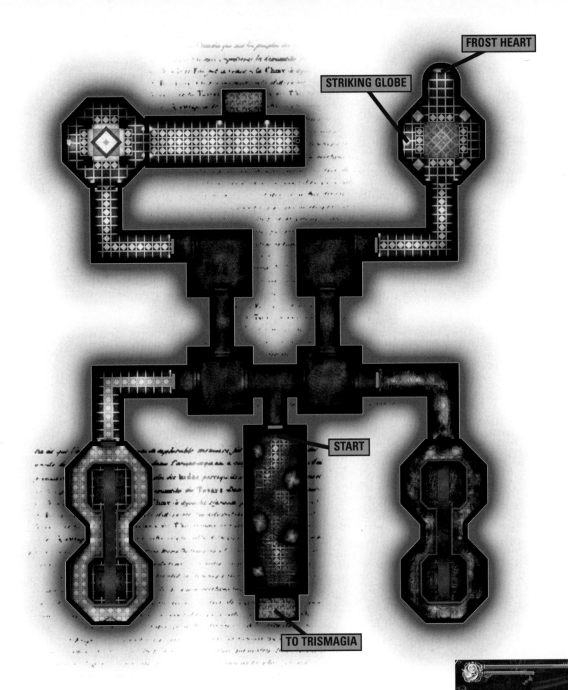

FROST HEART

STRIKING GLOBE

START

TO TRISMAGIA

HELL'S HALLWAY

Return to the connecting passage and navigate your way to the new area in the upper east corner of the in-game map, destroying Mortfinis along the way.

HALL OF THE GOAT CLAN

Proceed into the new room to discover several petrified Abyss Goats, poised and ready to attack. Strike the globe nearby until all purple white squares are turned purple, and the goats will come to life and attack. Two will tackle Dante on the ground, while the other two remain airborne and cover the zone with homing missiles. Use your Missile Launcher and Vendetta in combination to knock these tough creatures away as they come.

82

When all four Abyss Goats are toasted, move to the altar at the top of the room to obtain the **Frost Heart**. Now Dante can inflict cold attacks whenever he's in Devil Trigger.

PENTHOUSE ELEVATOR

The elevator to the top of the building quickly exceeds its maximum weight capacity when a dozen or more Mortfinis show up with an Abyss Goat. The Vendetta should help you clear this out this express to pain, but you'll still be dismantling caged skeletons long after the lift has stopped at the top floor.

Pick up the much-needed **Green Orb** and enter the penthouse to face the guardian of the ceremony.

TRISMAGIA

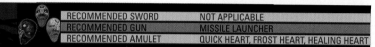

RECOMMENDED SWORD	NOT APPLICABLE
RECOMMENDED GUN	MISSILE LAUNCHER
RECOMMENDED AMULET	QUICK HEART, FROST HEART, HEALING HEART

The first few seconds of the battle, there is nothing to do but wait for Trismagia to separate into three faces, representing the elements of electricity, frost and flame. Because the three colored faces take so little damage from any type of gunfire it's more important to dodge attacks, rather than trying to attack the enemy.

While the three faces are taking their turns to attack, work on building your Devil Trigger gauges. Allowing Dante to get hit is one way to do it, because you can always regain lost vitality when the Healing Heart is equipped and you Devil Trigger. Sometimes the frost face will launch five large icicles that crash into the floor and stick out of the ground. Bash your way through these columns with the sword to fill your DT gauges quickly.

After the three faces have all had a significant number of turns to attack, they will reform into a single creature. Now it's Dante's turn to attack! When the single head appears and becomes a target, Devil Trigger and hold the ⬤ button to blast the lone face with ice attacks. Trismagia will prepare a devastating combo beam attack while you fire. Move to one side of the platform to see the approaching blast with better visibility, and Flip Escape out of harm's way. When Trismagia separates again, hit [L1] to turn off your Devil Trigger. Wait until the next time Trismagia unites, and perform the same attack again to finish the battle.

As the oracle's single vitality meter gets low, the icicles which crash onto Dante's platform become hard to destroy. The boss is using them as bait, so that Dante is busy slashing away while the boss sneaks up on him with an attack. Unfortunately, you won't be able to build your DT gauges this way anymore. To remove the icicles effectively, equip the Missile Launcher and blast two or three out of the way instantly.

When the boss is defeated step on the portal in the penthouse to be teleported to the building juncture.

MISSION COMPLETE!	
S RANK REQUIREMENTS	
CLEAR TIME	9:00 MINUTES
ORBS	7000
STYLISH AVERAGE	20 "SHOW TIME!!" COMBOS
DAMAGE	0
ITEM USED	NONE

MISSION 17

"Evil must be opposed and destroyed."

-Guidepost for the Hunters *Chapter 12 Clause 9*

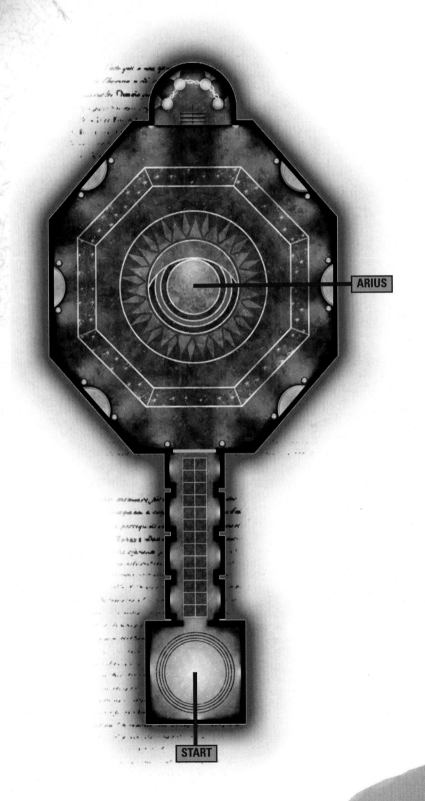

ARIUS, SECRETARY

RECOMMENDED SWORD	MERCILESS
RECOMMENDED ARSENAL	SHOTGUN
RECOMMENDED AMULET	AERIAL HEART, FROST HEART, HEALING HEART

Run through the corridor into the ceremony room for Dante's final showdown with Arius. Much like the last battle, the monsters that Arius summons to protect him are incidental. The battle ends when Arius himself is defeated. However, with his Secretaries serving as bodyguards, you're not going to get anywhere near the prince of darkness without defeating them first.

The two Secretaries employ some very familiar and deadly martial arts moves, using dual blades to attack. If they manage to hit Dante once, they can string up to eight attacks to the first! Therefore, getting anywhere near a Secretary is folly. Use the shotgun to blast them from a distance. Leap away from them and blast, and remember that Dante also holds a Handgun to perform Twosome Time. After you've knocked down a Secretary several times and have a filled a good portion of your Devil Trigger gauges, transform and blast one or both Secretaries right out of existence.

Arius loves to sit back and watch. He can usually be found on the sidelines, sitting on a throne and sipping wine while the chaos commences. He fires a random shot at Dante occasionally, and summons monkey demons in threes. Attack Jomothumsiras in the room until Dante's power gauges are refilled, then dash over to Arius and let him have some supercharged whacks with your sword. Avoid his usual spells, ignore the monkeys until they are needed to recharge power, and keep after the weakling coward until his human form finally gives out.

MISSION COMPLETE!	
S RANK REQUIREMENTS	
CLEAR TIME	4:00 MINUTES
ORBS	2000
STYLISH AVERAGE	10 "SHOW TIME!!" COMBOS
DAMAGE	0
ITEM USED	NONE

MISSION 18

"The hunter shall surpass all who came before him."

-Guidepost for the Hunters *Chapter 13 Clause 1*

ENTER CHARGED!

If luck is on your side, you'll have enough Red Orbs saved up to purchase a Purple Orb from the Power Up screen before starting this mission. Doing so allows you to enter the final boss fights with a longer Devil Trigger meter, fully charged!

ARGOSAX THE CHAOS

RECOMMENDED SWORD	MERCILESS
RECOMMENDED GUN	VARIOUS
RECOMMENDED AMULET	QUICK HEART, FROST HEART, HEALING HEART

Dante challenges the demon that Arius wished to replace. Argosax is a combination of Nefasturris, Orangguerra, Phantom, Jokatgulm, Furiataurus, and another blast from the past, the Griffon from the previous game. The idea is to work your way around the boss, taking on each individual section without drifting too far into another section's area. If so, you'll be dealing with two bosses at once instead of just one!

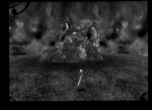

If you weren't able to purchase a Purple Orb before starting your mission, then one of your main goals during this battle is to fill your Devil Trigger gauges to be prepared for the next boss. Use only regular attacks as much as possible against Argosax, so that you're ready to face the final enemy afterward.

Start by defeating Nefasturris. Leap over its mouth beam attacks and Flip Escape away from the star pattern attacks. Blast it with the shotgun whenever you have an opportunity. The monster building crumbles when the vitality bar changes color.

Head to the left and use the Submachine Guns to challenge Orangguerra next. Trapped inside Argosax, the big monkey's only attack is to shoot force balls at Dante. By narrowly dodging each ball and firing between attacks, you can really build up a good stylish combo! But that aside, you may need to expend a little Devil Trigger power to get past this monster without a scratch. A short burst of superhuman power and an uninterrupted volley of fire from Devil Man's hands should sink Orangguerra in agony.

Limbless, the Phantom only attacks by firing meteorites from its mouth. It will also bury its head in the ground, which means that lava columns will soon erupt under Dante's feet. After dodging several of the Phantom's attacks, run at the head and strike it several times. The Phantom is the best creature to use in order to fill your Devil Trigger gauges.

The single tentacle of Jokatgulm is a puzzling foe, because if you stand in a certain spot and just keep blasting, the section will die off without ever hurting

you. Move back to the edge of the area, and move left until the tentacle swings. Jump over side-to-side swings, and try to remain just to the right of the tentacle. Keep blasting with the Shotgun until the section dies.

Furiataurus may look helpless half-stuck in Argosax, but this stubborn creature is as bull-headed as ever. Move to the left until the fire minotaur becomes a target, then move a few steps to the right whenever it looks like Dante is about to get hit with flame breath. Keep blasting the monster with the shotgun, and absolutely do not approach or you'll feel the bashing power of that big mace.

The Griffon launches all of its red lightning beam attacks, famous from the previous game. Between attacks, remain patient and tap the ⬤ button rapidly to hit the Griffon with Handgun fire. As horizontal lines of lighting fly at Dante, jump over low ones and the next line will be targeted at Dante's air height. That way, you can just walk under the next line, and only have to dodge the low beams. The Griffon also fires two beams out to the sides, which converge on Dante. Learn to recognize this attack quickly and just jump straight into the air to avoid it. The hard attack to dodge is the curtain of vertical lightning rods that zoom across the ground. You must wait until the absolute last second before the wall of red electricity is going to hit Dante, then Flip Escape to either side. Once you get through curtain, the timing of when to flip should be easily learned.

Make wise use of the Green Orbs in four locations around the area. Avoid using them if you can, so that they are still available during the next tough battle. Avoid the temptation to Devil Trigger in order to end this long battle more quickly. The only way you can avoid using a Vital Star or Devil Star in the next battle is by entering fully charged and prepared!

THE DESPAIR EMBODIED

RECOMMENDED SWORD	REBELLION
RECOMMENDED GUN	HANDGUNS
RECOMMENDED AMULET	QUICK HEART, FROST HEART, HEALING HEART

Quickly enter the Status menu as the last section of Argosax collapses and equip Dante according to the guidelines above. The sex changing, teleporting fire angel has so many attacks, it's not even worth describing. The only strategy you need to follow is to Devil Trigger, rush the boss, and attack with your sword as much as possible. If Despair disappears and resumes attacking from a short distance away, press ⬤ to blast him until you can move close enough to attack him with your sword again. If Despair flies into the air, quickly enter the Status menu and switch to the Aerial Heart. Fly up to its level and hit it several times with Round Trip.

When Devil Trigger expires, do your best to avoid attacks that seemingly can't be avoided, and attack whenever it gives you any opening. Taking several hits of damage from something like Despair's homing missile attack will fill the Devil Trigger gauges swiftly. Vitality lost can be recovered when Dante Devil Triggers while equipped with the Healing Heart. As soon as the gauges are filled to the second or third line, wait for Despair to reappear near Dante, Devil Trigger and attack again. Keep repeating that process, and you should be able to wear down whatever's left of its vitality bar pretty quickly.

MISSION COMPLETE!

S RANK REQUIREMENTS	
CLEAR TIME	5:00 MINUTES
ORBS	2000
STYLISH AVERAGE	15 "SHOW TIME!!" COMBOS
DAMAGE	0
ITEM USED	NONE

I THINK THE DEVIL IS ABOUT TO CRY

Vanquishing Despair, there's nothing left for Dante to do but head straight to Hell. But that's a story for another day. Completing one game of **Devil May Cry 2** is like licking the tip from the top of an ice cream cone, meaning you've barely scratched the surface of this game.

PATH 2: THE PROTECTOR

LUCIA

Though the protector may be skilled and trained for survival, she is not prepared for the horrors that the armies of evil have in store, nor the dark secrets, which may be unleashed. The foresight of her mother and seer is contained in the following pages. Use the information contained herein to determine the righteous path to redemption.

COMBAT MASTERY

For centuries following the dawn of mankind, the islands of Vidu Mali stood as a monument to a great treachery forced upon the fledgling humans by the devils. Since that dark page in the history of the world, the islands of Vidu Mali were cleared of demonic influence and protected from that time by a race of heroic half-demon women. Lucia is the descendant of this line of heavenly protectors sworn to safeguard the sanctity of the islands, uphold the peaceful lives of the townsfolk, and secure the shrines wherein the Arcana once used to defeat the demons long ago are sealed.

Lucia has been training under the guidance of her mother and fellow Vidu Mali protector, Matier. Although her skills are still developing, the demons have suddenly invaded Vidu Mali once again. Matier feared this would happen, since the arrival of the evil sorcerer Arius several years before, and the subsequent building of the triumvirate skyscrapers, which house his diabolical Auroboros Corporation on the northern island. Now Matier must find a way to protect Vidu Mali from evil once again, but she is too old and her protégé is not yet skilled enough to take on someone as powerful as Arius.

Matier summons the legendary devil hunter, Dante. Having known his father Sparda in previous years, she is certain that his skills will be necessary to stop the evil and prevent the demon world from consuming our dimension. While Dante takes on the devils of Arius directly, Matier sends her daughter Lucia to the shrines of Arcana throughout Vidu Mali, in an effort to secure the ceremonial items before they fall into the hands of evil.

BASIC SKILLS

Lucia employs two lethal short swords and a bevy of various throwing weapons to protect her home islands from the forces of ultimate corruption. All of her basic moves are detailed in this section, presenting opportunities to continue a stylish combo once it has been sparked.

Throwing Blades

Lucia begins her missions loaded with an endless supply of handcrafted silver Throwing Daggers, which she deploys in rapid-fire succession. Press ⬡ to toss blades at targeted enemies. Tap ⬡ rapidly to throw them at a higher rate.

When Lucia jumps high into the sky, the duration of the jump can be suspended by throwing from midair. Lucia gains a brief aerial advantage over opponents on the ground by tossing blades from above. While in the air, rapidly tap ☐ to make Lucia toss projectiles hand-over-hand during her descent. Since this move allows Lucia to fling blades much more quickly, you'll want to spend many of her battles remaining airborne.

Weapons with a lower firing rate, such as the Darts and Cranky Bombs, will fire only two or three times during a single jump. With the Darts equipped, press ☐ with the proper timing during a jump to throw a fan-shaped volley of Darts at enemies directly below.

Sword Combo

Press △ to use Lucia's swords. In addition to defeating enemies, her swords are useful for destroying breakable objects in the environment—such as statues and furniture. Sometimes hidden orbs are released as a result. Certain key objects, such as blue globes, must be struck repeatedly with swords until they activate to unlock new areas of the environment.

By pressing △ repeatedly, Lucia will perform myriad vertical and horizontal sword slashes, followed by a spinning slash finish. This combination of sword strokes can be modified to include powerful kicks when the Left Analog Stick is moved in a certain direction with the right timing. Such moves might spark a stylish combo, and so they are listed in the following section.

Flip Escape

Press ○ to make Lucia roll forward. Rolling is useful for moving Lucia to another position quickly, such as avoiding enemy attacks. You might also try rolling if you want to dive for a Red Orb that's about to expire and disappear. Used in combination with blade tossing, rolling can be used to maintain a stylish combo as you get closer to an enemy. Pressing the Left Analog Stick in any direction can influence the direction of the roll.

Jumping

Press ✗ to jump in the air. The direction of the jump can be modified while in midair by pressing the Left Analog Stick after ✗ is pressed. Use this midair control function to hop onto low platforms and ledges.

By pressing the left stick in any direction at the moment ✗ is pressed, you can make Lucia flip in midair. This move will carry her farther through the air in the given direction.

Air Hike

After jumping, press ✗ while Lucia is in midair to double-jump. When the Air Hike is performed without use of the Left Analog Stick, Lucia leaps straight up and then performs a back flip. If you press the Left Analog Stick in any direction during the first or second jump of the Air Hike, Lucia will flip in that direction. For careful jumps onto higher platforms and ledges, jump straight up and press the Left Analog Stick during the second jump to control Lucia's direction.

Kick Jump

While moving toward or facing a wall, press ✗ to jump and then press it again while holding the Left Analog Stick toward the wall. At the height of the first leap, Lucia makes contact with the wall and then springs upward like a cat to gain extra height. This is the move to use for leaping up a series of ledges.

Wall Hike

While facing a wall, press ○ to start a wall hike. Lucia runs up the wall, then back flips away from the surface and lands a few yards away. This is a very effective method to avoid getting cornered by enemies.

A Wall Hike allows Lucia to reach a higher level than an initial jump off the ground, such as at the start of a Kick Jump. Also, when Lucia back flips off the wall, press ✗ while she is in midair to add a second jump to the move. Moving the Left Analog Stick simultaneously can control the direction of the second jump.

Wall Run

In a slight variation, press ○ while running alongside a wall to perform a Wall Run. Lucia continues moving forward while running up onto the vertical surface. After a few twisting hops where she becomes completely horizontal, she leaps off the wall and flips in midair to fling herself forward before landing.

A second jump can also be added to this move by pressing ✗ after Lucia leaps off the wall. Move the Left Analog Stick at the moment ✗ is pressed to control the direction of the second jump.

Swimming

Several of Lucia's missions require her to swim and survive underwater for the duration. Lucia does not require a constant supply of oxygen, so running out of air is not a problem. Swimming is much like flying, and Lucia will slowly sink to the bottom whether she is moving or not. Move the Left Analog Stick to swim through the water, and hold ✗ to avoid sinking further. Tap ✗ rapidly to swim upward in a smooth motion. Hold ○ while swimming to swiftly descend.

SPECIAL MOVES

In addition to the basic moves that Lucia performs like a pro, she also has secret combat attacks and sexy moves that enable her to generate and improve stylish combos. All of the moves listed in this section have the ability to start a stylish combo, or to raise an already existing combo to the next level.

Twist Escape

While fighting an enemy, hold ⟦R1⟧ to lock on. Move the Left Analog Stick to Lucia's left or right, and press ○. The protector skips and spins toward the given direction. If you hold ⟦R1⟧, move the left stick away from the foe, and press ○ - she back flips away. A brief moment of invulnerability occurs while Lucia is in motion, so this move can be used to dodge right past projectiles and attacks. If a Twist Escape is executed successfully at the instant an attack misses, it could spark or improve a stylish combo.

Sky High (Short)

While facing an enemy, hold ⓡ⒈ and move the Left Analog Stick *away* from the foe. Press Ⓐ simultaneously, and Lucia kicks the enemy into

the air. At this point, you can leap into the air beside them and kick them back down to the ground, or you can whip out some knives and try to juggle the helpless foe in midair. This is the shorter version of Sky High.

Sky High (Complete)

The complete version of Sky High is initiated by holding ⓡ⒈ while moving the Left Analog Stick away from the enemy, then pressing Ⓐ *hard* so that when Lucia kicks the opponent - she flies up into the air beside them. Continue holding ⓡ⒈, and with the proper timing press Ⓐ to make Lucia double-kick her opponent while both are airborne. Another Ⓐ press with the right timing causes her to spin kick the poor monster again. Finally, press Ⓐ a final time, and Lucia will smash the enemy to the ground by flipping and hitting the enemy with the back of her leg. All of this occurs in split sec-

onds while in midair! This is a tricky move to execute, but mercilessly attacking a helpless foe three times in the air without allowing them to fall is brilliant.

Front Walkover

While facing the enemy, hold ⓡ⒈ and move the Left Analog Stick *toward* the opponent, and then press Ⓐ. Lucia flips forward on her hands and delivers two hard kicks to the enemy's sternum or groin. This move is highly effective for knocking most foes off their feet and starting a stylish combo. Executed with proper timing, Lucia can perform this move continuously for as long as you desire.

Multiple Kick

Hold the Left Analog Stick *away* from the target while pressing Ⓐ to deliver a flurry of kicks to an opponent, without the use of swords. It seems that while enemies might be more resilient against Lucia's blades, *all* foes can be knocked to the ground by her kick attacks.

Aerial Walkover

Start a normal Sword Combo, and move the Left Analog Stick *toward or away* from the enemy after the first double-slash. Lucia will finish with two swift kicks, a leg sweep and an aerial walkover finale. This is a fantastic move for finishing off enemies that are already on the ground.

Leg Blade

Jump or Air Hike upward, and press Ⓐ as Lucia flips at the top of her leap to come down upon an enemy directly below with a crushing assault. Lucia uses the back of her leg to flatten enemies to the ground, for instant death or easy disposal.

Twosome Time

While nailing a target with an endless succession of Throwing Daggers, enemies may attempt to ambush Lucia from the side or behind. As the second enemy approaches, increase your rate of knife delivery on the targeted enemy by tapping 🔲 rapidly, then move the Left Analog Stick toward the enemy approaching from close behind or to the side of Lucia. She will whip a single dagger at the foe hard enough to knock them several feet away.

This move might be easier to execute if you lock on to the prime target by holding ⓡ⒈, then move the Left Analog Stick toward the oncoming foe. There is a slight chance while performing any of these defensive throws that Lucia will strike up or improve the level of a stylish combo.

Rapid Fire

Air Hike high into the air directly beside an enemy, and hold ⓡ⒈ to lock on. Move the left stick toward the foe, and tap Ⓐ rapidly. With any luck, Lucia will connect with the same set of kicks

she employs in the full Sky High move described above. This is a great way to meet Abyss Goats head-on in the sky, or to take apart a Sargasso floating some feet off the floor.

Lush

One of Lucia's more amazing moves is tricky to pull off and requires some timing. Jump or Air Hike above an enemy and hold ⓡ⒈ to lock on. The instant that Lucia touches the ground, press Ⓐ.

With a fair sense of timing, you'll cause her to spin on her hands and kick all enemies in a tight circle around her!

DEVIL TRIGGER

Lucia is capable of utilizing the heritage of her half-demon ancestry, transforming into a white-feathered, winged demon that actually resembles a more angelic incarnation. The term "Devil Trigger" refers to this state of transformation, as well as the power that is contained in the meter. All of Lucia's attacks gain a tremendous amount of power while she is transformed. Lucia gains the ability to perform certain special attacks that are only available while Devil Trigger lasts.

However, because of her half-human lineage, this transformation can be maintained for only a short duration. Once the power contained in the Devil Trigger gauges runs out, Lucia reverts to her normal form and level of strength.

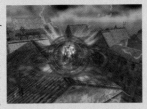

By equipping magical stones in her amulet, Lucia gains certain powers and abilities while "in" Devil Trigger. These stones enable her to use the magical elements of fire, ice, and electricity against opponents with her attacks. She can also gain the ability to fly through the air, run across the ground at ten times normal speed, or even swim faster than the most adept deep sea predator. Devil Trigger can also be used to regain vitality and stop time. All the details are contained in the **Devilish Tools** chapter.

Lucia starts each mission with a full vitality bar and empty Devil Trigger gauges. Savagery in all forms is food for the devils, and so for every point of damage Lucia inflicts or sustains, her Devil Trigger gauges are built up a little bit. Devil Trigger can also be recharged by using a Devil Star item, or by purchasing a Purple Orb to extend the length of the meter before a mission. As the Devil Trigger gauge is elongated, Lucia becomes able to remain in this hyperactive state for longer periods of time.

When the Devil Trigger gauges are gray, Lucia cannot transform. Once the gauge turns a certain color, representing the elemental stone of power equipped in the amulet, press ⬛ to enter Devil Trigger. Lucia can usually transform when the Devil Trigger meter fills up to the first gauge line.

Running

While in Devil Trigger, Lucia runs at a much higher speed than normal. Crossing long distances requires less time if Devil Trigger can be used to move. When the Quick Heart is obtained during the game and equipped in the amulet, the movement speed of Devil Trigger is increased further! With the Quick Heart, Lucia can cross incredibly long distances in a matter of seconds rather than a whole minute. Speed is also integral in escaping from enemies or running behind them before they can target or follow Lucia.

Baton Twirl

While Lucia is in Devil Trigger and fighting an opponent, repeatedly press △ to begin a Sword Combo. After the second swing, move the Left Analog Stick toward or away from the direction Lucia is facing and continue pressing △. Lucia steps and delivers a series of thrusts instead of swings, then spins her blades inside an enemy's torso.

Feathered Fury

While Lucia is in Devil Trigger and fighting an opponent, press △ repeatedly to begin a Sword Combo. After the third swing, move the Left Analog Stick toward or away from the direction Lucia faces and rapidly tap △ until the combination ends. After a few sword strokes and a single walkover kick, Lucia plants herself in front of a foe and slashes back and forth in berserk style fighting. She then flips backward and kicks dirt in her opponents' eyes!

Flying

Devil Trigger Lucia gains the ability to hover and soar through the air after obtaining the Aerial Heart during the course of her missions. Air Hike high into the air and Devil Trigger while the Aerial Heart is equipped. Lucia spreads her wings and begins to slowly descend if you do not act. Move the Left Analog Stick to fly across the area. Press ✕ to ascend straight upward, and tap ✕ repeatedly to continue rising. Hold ✕ while moving the Left Analog Stick and Lucia will maintain a certain altitude above the ground. To descend at a slightly faster rate than the usual, hold ◯ while hovering or flying.

There are limitations to flying, as Lucia will rise to only a certain height above the surface. In some areas, this limitation is disabled for a special reason, and you can fly up several levels to the top of a large chamber if you desire. However, flying in Devil Trigger is prohibited in areas where a good deal of platform jumping is required.

Certain attacks become available only when Lucia is in Devil Trigger **and** flying off the ground.

Air Raid

While flying in Devil Trigger, press and hold □ to release a fan shaped array of magic darts that will attack multiple opponents on either side before homing in upon the main target. Lay your thumb over □ and ✕ simultaneously, so that Lucia maintains altitude while shooting.

Dual Slash

While flying in Devil Trigger, press △ to attack an aerial or tall opponent with both of Lucia's magic endowed blades. This attack can also be used to quickly activate a key globe object that is floating in the air during Lucia's Mission 2.

WEAPONS

SWORDS

Melee attacks are the key to striking stylish combos and dealing the most damage. Additionally, attacking enemies with swords fills the Devil Trigger gauges of either hero much faster than gunfire. However, this style of combat requires the most precision, and a firm knowledge of the weapons available to the devil hunters.

Improving Swords

All swords start off at Level 1, and upgrades can be purchased at any God of Time statue or in the Power Up screen before a mission. Swords have five levels, so while the first upgrade is relatively low in cost, improving a sword to its maximum level is a costly venture overall. The higher the level of the sword, the greater its attack power is and the sooner it will strike a stylish combo. Since swords provide the start of all stylish combos, increasing their level takes precedence over improving the levels of firearms or throwing weapons.

SWORD ENHANCEMENTS	
LEVEL	**RED ORB COST**
LV1	0
LV2	5000
LV3	10000
LV4	20000
LV5	40000

CUTLASEER

The regular weapons of Lucia are a set of short, curved blades. For use in the execution of master martial arts combinations against enemies, these stylish weapons enable Lucia to slash away at enemies on all sides. In choosing a weapon for Lucia, the Cutlaseers work best against swift but strong enemies such as Agonofinis and their stronger brothers, plus all types of Msira.

KLYAMOOR

When the enemies are swift and elusive, Lucia must carry swords that swing fast and wide. The Klyamoors are effective against low-vitality enemies that often try to get away rather than suffer her melee blows, such as all types of spell casters, Puia, and Sargassos.

ZAMBAK

The Zambak are a heavy set of machetes, for use in hacking up taller enemies with thick shells or strong constitutions. However, they are slightly slower to swing due to their weight, so their incredible striking power cannot be used against all types of enemies efficiently. The Zambaks are best employed against tall goat-headed demons, Savage Golems, and Demonochorus lying on the ground.

ARSENAL

Whereas swords and special moves are the starting point of any stylish combo, a good devil hunter needs the rapid-fire power to carry it through. After striking a stylish combo and defeating any enemy, blast away with these firearms and thrown projectiles to keep those lovely colored words onscreen. The entire game can be won simply by shooting foes, but it's a long and hard road. Use all weapons in the characters' arsenal in combination with melee swords to eliminate foes efficiently and stylishly.

Improving Guns and Projectiles

Side arms and thrown weapons all have only two levels. Improving the characters' secondary weapons takes a back seat to enhancing their swords, which are the tools used to strike stylish combos. Level 1 Handguns can sustain a stylish combo just as well as when they're at Level 3. However, once you manage to improve an arsenal weapon, you'll find that your characters have greater stopping power against larger foes and flying enemies in addition to inflicting more damage.

ARSENAL ENHANCEMENTS

LEVEL	RED ORB COST
LV1	0
LV2	10000
LV3	30000

THROWING DAGGERS

There's no telling where she keeps them, but Lucia carries an endless supply of tiny hand-carved silver ceremonial knives for use against the demon kind. Press □ rapidly to deliver a barrage of knives into any standing or airborne target. Try Lucia's airborne move, where she twists and flings daggers hand-over-hand so rapidly, even goat-headed demons start to shake in their hooves. While standing in a group of enemies, Lucia will toss daggers at foes approaching from the side or rear, hard enough to knock them off their feet. The easiest of Lucia's arsenal to use, the Throwing Daggers are good for almost any enemy throughout her missions.

DARTS

Tiny blades that fit between Lucia's knuckles, these Darts are thrown in clusters at time. The result is a cone-shaped spread of projectiles, that damages all enemies in a broad range standing in front of Lucia. Also, if Lucia Air Hikes high enough above the enemies, she will fling a Dart cluster straight down at enemies directly below her with the right timing. However, because of the skill required in aligning the Darts between her fingers and throwing multiple blades from both hands simultaneously, it is too much to ask Lucia to perform this attack rapidly. Always be prepared to dodge while tossing the darts, and maintain a fair distance from the intended targets while doing so. This weapon is ineffective if only one blade hits its mark.

CRANKY BOMB

Lucia lights up the neighborhood with this short range, high-density explosive. When she is standing still, Lucia will toss the Cranky Bomb at the ground and slide backward. Any foe that touches the bomb will be blow sky high. This approach is great for enemies that do not have leaping capabilities. Lucia will also toss bombs at targeted foes simply by pressing the Left Analog Stick in the direction of the enemy as you press □. Bombs thrown high that manage to contact their target will explode on impact. If the bomb misses, it will remain on the ground a few seconds before exploding automatically. The blast from these bombs will not affect Lucia in the slightest, so feel free to set as many on the ground as quickly as you wish. However, using these at close range lowers visibility due to the cloud of smoke they expel upon detonation. Also, with a low accuracy rate this weapon can be quite tricky to use. However, when you manage to toss a Cranky Bomb right at the goat head of a demon and watch the whole brood flattened in one shot, it's well worth the effort and practice! Cranky bombs can also be used underwater, like miniature depth charges that explode just a few seconds after contact with the seafloor.

BOW GUN

Lucia spends several of her missions deep underwater, so it's important for her to have an applicable weapon. The Cranky Bombs tend to be a difficult weapon to use underwater, so the Bow Gun provides Lucia with a means of more direct attack. Lucia must stop swimming in order to fire the Bow Gun. Tap □ repeatedly to fire short volleys of small harpoons that can pierce even the thick scales of underwater demons such as Blades. A smart strategy is to swim to a new position between volleys, so that Lucia is not a sitting duck in the water. Because it's used so little in the course of the entire game, the Bow Gun is much easier to improve than all the other weapons.

BOW GUN ENHANCEMENTS

LEVEL	RED ORB COST
LV1	0
LV2	4000
LV3	8000

MISSION 1

"Dispatched on a mission to gather the Arcana sought by the forces of evil, the descendant of the ancient half-demon clan must prevent the hand of the wicked from crushing the innocent. The threat of devils leads her away from her outpost, to the sound of the chimes. Toward the south, the protector will find the time."

-Guidepost for the Protectors *Chapter 1 Clause 3*

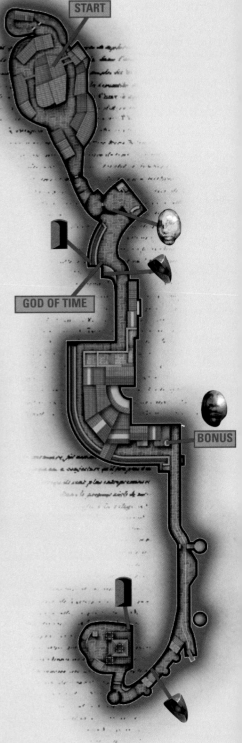

BEGINNER'S MODE

Lucia's missions act as a side-story to Dante's main quest. Many of her missions are shorter and less complex than Dante's, and so her game is easier to complete. If you're having trouble in Dante's missions, this might be a better place to start. However, playing through Lucia's disc first will spoil some aspects of Dante's story!

OFFERING OF ORBS

To unseal the door at the south end of the villa area, Lucia must gather enough Red Orbs to get to the next area. Step forward to the right and smash the smokestack on the roof. A single **Red Orb** is gained. Head back to the cottage to acquire a string of orbs, then proceed to search the streets and alleys for orbs. Slash all the smokestacks to collect the hidden Red Orbs. Press **R1** to check the number of orbs acquired.

Over 60 Red Orbs can be gathered in this first area.

Be wary of living door seals such as this. They could cause you great harm.

ARENA OF PAIN

Up the path and through the arch on the left, Lucia encounters a rash of the demons that have been plaguing her homeland. Press ☐ to toss Throwing Daggers at the Agonofinis in rapid succession, or press △ to engage in martial arts combos

mixed with sword attacks. Anyone who has played through Dante's game already should be able to quickly adapt to Lucia's unique fighting style.

AGONOFINIS

Trapped in their torturous cages, these lilting and staggering creatures are hardly a challenge for someone with Dante's arsenal and skills. Encased entirely in metal, they are weak against lightning attacks utilizing the Electro Heart. The most dangerous types are the disc-throwing variety, so eliminate them first whenever Agonofinis are encountered.

While taking down slow and lumbering enemies such as Agonofinis should be quite simple, striking a stylish combo is a bit more specific in regard to Lucia's moves. A martial arts move is required to spark a stylish combo. The words "Don't Worry" will appear onscreen after performing attacks such as **Sky High** (Lock on with **R1**, press the Left Analog Stick away from enemy and then press △), or the **Front Walkover** (Lock on with **R1**, press the Left Analog Stick toward enemy and then press △) or the **Leg Blade** (while falling from a jump, press △ hard). The words can be kept onscreen by using the **Throwing Daggers** (hold ▢), performing a **Flip Escape** ○, or by regular melee attacks.

Moves such as the Multiple Kick (press the Left Analog Stick away from enemy, tap △ rapidly) and the **Lush** (while falling from a jump, hold **R1**, press △ upon landing) could improve the level of the combo, so that the words onscreen change from yellow to red, eventually resulting in "Show Time!!" As the level of the stylish combo rises, more orbs will be released for each enemy killed. The fast way to improve the strength of weapons is to go for a stylish combo every time. This first enemy group is a small set, but you can definitely reach "Show Time!!" before they call it quits.

HIGH JUMP

After eliminating the demon cluster, jump high in the area to locate an opening high on the south wall. **Air Hike** (Press ✕ after first jump) upward to grab the two Red Orbs and the **Gold Orb** suspended in air then jump again if needed to leap through the opening.

Gold Orbs automatically resurrect Lucia if she is killed. She can carry only one at a time.

THE GOD OF TIME AND THE HIDDEN CHAMBER

Above a small rise to the left of the God of Time floats a **Blue Orb Fragment**.

Proceed down the street to find a God of Time statue, which functions as a shop to use during missions. Due to the time constraints of each mission, it's wiser to improve weapons and buy usable items through the "Power Up" option before each mission starts. However, during your first game you'll hardly be worried about ranking.

Jump over the low wall into the channel running alongside the street. At one end of the chasm is a Red Orb. If you check the sewer grate just below the God of Time statue, Lucia will enter a hidden room full of demons. By finding these Secret Rooms and defeating the demons in the room, Lucia might gain Blue Orb Fragments. When four of these fragments form a whole Blue Orb, Lucia's vitality meter will be increased. Every Secret Room awards the player with Green Orbs and White Orbs that restore vitality and Devil Trigger power respectively, so it's always worth it!

SECRET ROOM LOCATION 1

Drop into the gully next to the God of Time statue, and check the grate at the south end to find the first Secret Room.

CLEARING THE STREETS

Continue past the God of Time up the stairs and smash the bench to obtain a Red Orb. Defeat another set of Agonofinis, and then jump onto the rooftops to the left. Cross over to the balcony and smash a bench plus some gargoyle statues to obtain more Red Orbs.

SKY BATTLE

Proceed across the rooftops until the evil vulture demons from the initial cinematic reappear. Now is the best time to see what kind of midair shot Lucia is. Air Hike high into the sky above the shingles and tap ▭ rapidly. Twisting in midair, Lucia flings an endless barrage of Throwing Daggers with grace and ease. Most of the attacks of the flying Puia are directed at the ground, so the sky is the best place for Lucia to meet these bird creatures head-on. However, avoid leaping into the sky if a Puia is hovering overhead nearby, or it will head butt Lucia and fling her to the ground!

The street signs can be smashed to receive Red Orbs.

At the north end of the channel beside the long street is a Red Orb.

Two more Red Orbs can be collected in a small alcove formed by the roof sections, far back among the buildings.

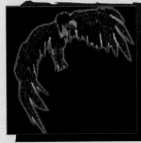

PUIA

These feathered fiends can fire missiles and swoop down to hit characters on the ground, but they're weak against attacks from the air. Puia are very easy to kill, and only become a nuisance when coupled with stronger types of devils.

HIDDEN ORB BONUSES

Jump over the low wall to collect a small Red Orb, and proceed up to the square. A round column stands at the corner in front of a tall building. If you can jump so that Lucia lands directly in the center of this column, **Bonus Red Orbs** drop out of nowhere. There are many locations in the game where a plethora of extra orbs can be made to appear by landing on a high platform or ledge. Basically, if you see a high surface that might be hard to reach, jump to it!

Drop into the chasm behind the bridge to collect four large Red Orbs.

SAVAGE GOLEMS

Proceed up the street, dismantling another set of Agonofinis. Be especially wary of the caged skeletons that sling rounded blades across long areas, like boomeranging buzz saws. Pay close attention to the hands of Agonofinis enemies as they appear, figure out what weapons they carry and slay the disc throwers first.

SAVAGE GOLEM

Although extremely tough with doubled vitality meters, these lumbering brutes move extremely slowly. When attacked at close range, they will project long blue spikes tipped with poison to pierce their enemy. They can also extend their limbs under the earth to surprise their prey from underneath with this type of attack. Poison will continuously lower Dante's vitality until either a Holy Star is used or the effect expires. To defeat a Savage Golem, weaken it with constant gunfire. Then use strong sword attacks to hack off the arms and upper torso. When the legs are flung into the corner, things aren't over yet. Lock on to the flailing legs and shoot them until the vitality is wholly depleted, or the monster will regenerate its upper torso and lost limbs and recovering full vitality!

Proceeding up the street, Lucia is enclosed in a small area with a slow but deadly brute known as a Savage Golem. Before launching into any melee attacks, wear the creature down a bit by tossing Throwing Daggers at it safely from a distance. When chunks of the creature start to fly off, rush it and attack with a bevy of sword attacks. Chop off arms and sections of the upper torso before the creature manages to seize or hit Lucia. Try to keep it off balance with your blows, so that it cannot metamorphose into a prickly pear of poison spikes. If Lucia is poisoned, she'll turn a lavender color and her vitality gauge will continually decrease for several moments. When what little is left of the Savage Golem's lower torso flops on the ground, resume pelting it with Throwing Daggers. If the legs manage to scamper away to a safe place, the whole creature will regenerate with full vitality! A second Savage Golem appears just as the first is evaporating. Lather, rinse, and repeat.

THE RACE FOR TIME

Continue toward the base of the clock tower after eliminating the poisonous brutes. Inside the archway, press the Left Analog Stick toward the right wall and press ○ to start a Wall Hike. As Lucia back flips off the wall, press ✕ while midair to Air Hike upward to the apex of the arch. Grab the Red Orb at the top.

Notice the large monument carved from the stone on the right wall. Jump toward the wall, and then press ✕ at the zenith of the jump while the character is facing the surface. Like a cat, Lucia will bounce off the wall and flip onto the monument's shoulder. Face the head, and hold the Left Analog Stick to the right as you jump just once. Done correctly, Lucia should flip right onto the monument's head and find a **Blue Orb Fragment**.

Jump over the low gate, grabbing a Red Orb on top. At the next corner, move to the left; drop through an unseen doorway and into the ruins of a small watchtower. A large Red Orb is gained this way.

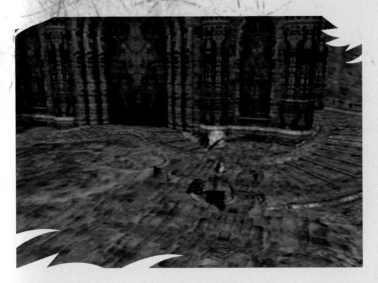

Continue up the stairs to the base of the clock tower, smashing the gargoyle statues for more Red Orbs. Touching the doors of the clock tower ends the mission, but you should check around the side of the building for a Secret Room first.

SECRET ROOM LOCATION 2

Move into the narrow area to the left of the clock tower doors, and search the area under the ugly face on the wall to enter the next level Secret Room.

MISSION COMPLETE!	
S RANK REQUIREMENTS	
CLEAR TIME	9:00 MINUTES
ORBS	4000
STYLISH AVERAGE	6 "SHOW TIME!!" COMBOS
DAMAGE	0
ITEM USED	NONE

MISSION 2

"One key to the demon world is being guarded in a tower, until the master comes to claim it. Also within the tower is a gem of power against the devils. The aerial heart will give the protector the chance to reach the skies. Activating the machinery awakens the prisoner who serves evil against its will."

-Guidepost for the Protectors *Chapter 1 Clause 8*

ALTAR OF THE GOAT DEMONS

Move away from the door, because remaining near it for too long will trigger a large hand which can hurt Lucia! In the corner to her left is a Devil Trigger Recharge Plate. Step on the plate, and your empty DT gauges will be instantly filled. It's important to enter the imminent battle prepared.

GOATLING

Goatlings are strong enemies that have some flight ability. On the ground, they charge at Dante and attempt to bash him aside with powerful claw swipes. The best technique for fighting a Goatling on the ground is to shoot it until it begins to convulse, then bash it off its feet with a powerful sword attack such as the Spin Bash. Once it's down, keep it from getting back up with continuous gunfire or sword chops. While hovering in air, a Goatling will charge and release powerful homing missiles that Dante must dodge using jumps or the Flip Escape (●). Dante is weak against this attack if he jumps up to the Goatling's level, so stay on the ground and blast the creature out of the sky with a barrage of bullets. Multiple Goatlings make survival extremely difficult, so good luck.

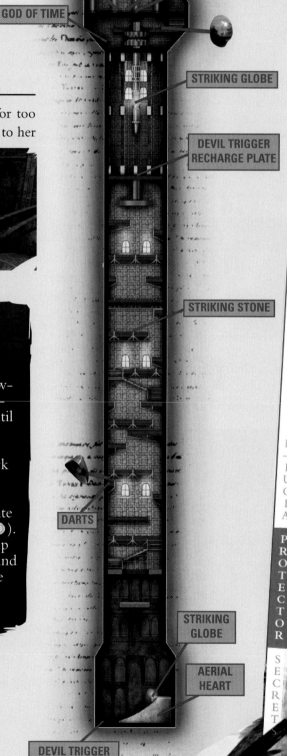

TARTUSSIAN

ARCANA SPADA

GOD OF TIME

STRIKING GLOBE

DEVIL TRIGGER RECHARGE PLATE

STRIKING STONE

DARTS

STRIKING GLOBE

AERIAL HEART

DEVIL TRIGGER RECHARGE PLATE

Run up both sets of stairs, collecting all the little Red Orbs dotting the rises. Between the stairs is a sealed capsule where a stone for Lucia's amulet lies. To obtain the stone, you must strike the globe on the balcony until all of the white squares surrounding it are converted to purple.

As you might have feared, activating the globe causes the two giant goat statues to come to life. One Goatling will remain aloft, and fires homing missiles at Lucia. The other giant will drop to the ground and charge. Goatlings are best handled by starting off with strong kicks such as Sky High or Front Walkover. Once you have knocked a Goatling on their back, don't let them get up! Keep hitting them with Throwing Daggers until you can get close enough to do another melee attack to finish it off. For the one remaining in the air, jump up and kick it several times in midair with the Rapid Fire move (Hold R1 , Left Analog Stick toward foe, tap △). If you're not finding the battle so easy, feel free to use Lucia's Devil Trigger since the Recharge Plate is nearby.

AERIAL HEART

Defeating the two Goatlings, the seal on the altar breaks. Approach to receive the **Aerial Heart**. With this stone equipped in the Amulet, Lucia can fly to great heights by pressing ✕ while in Devil Trigger. To descend while flying, hold ◯ .

Dispatch a group of interloping Agonofinis, then Devil Trigger and steadily tap ✕ to rise to the ceiling. At the midpoint of the tall walls, be sure to grab the Red Orb in the corner. Continue flying up to the ceiling before Lucia's gauges empty. Air Hike upward through the gap in the ceiling to the next level.

DANGEROUS PLATFORMS

Avoid knocking the enemies off the platform, or you'll have to drop a few levels to clean them up.

Run up the steps and leap onto the large square platform. A double-trio of Agonofinis will appear one set at a time. If you fail to get off this large platform within 3 seconds after destroying the last cage skeleton, two more sets will materialize. On the other hand, this is a great place to do a lot of fighting and build your orb supply, if that's what you're after.

Kick Jump up the wall on the right to a small platform with a gargoyle. Smash the statue to obtain the **Darts**, which damage all enemies in a cone-shaped area in front of Lucia. However, they fire more slowly than the Throwing Daggers. Lucia's arsenal can be switched out quickly by pressing L2 when the protector is standing on the ground or between attacks.

Kick Jump to the left of the platform to obtain a **Blue Orb Fragment**!

THE STRIKING STONE

Look for ledges to jump to, and keep going up the tower by levels. Dismantle another set of Agonofinis on a square platform, and leap off quickly before another group appears. The next large plank is blessedly free of enemies, and a glowing stone hovers just above the boards. This is a Striking Stone, where your character can obtain a great quantity of Red Orbs by slashing the stone quickly and repeatedly with swords. However, if you tap ⚠ too rapidly, Lucia will go into her full sword combo and sail right past the stone. After the first strike, you have only a short amount of time to keep gathering orbs before the stone runs dry. To get the most out of a Striking Stone, press ⚠ only at short intervals so that Lucia does the first two attacks of her combo. With the right timing, you can keep repeating the first two attacks and get more orbs from the stone.

Smash the gargoyle on the platform just above the Striking Stone to obtain a Red or Green Orb, depending on your current vitality level.

A Red Orb hangs suspended in space near the top. If you jump for it, Lucia will drop several levels down. Double jump and Devil Trigger while midair. Glide over to the orb, and then rise up through the hole in the ceiling to the next level.

MACHINA DE CHRONOS

Smash the gargoyles on either side of the room for Red Orbs and fill your Devil Trigger gauges by walking carefully onto the DT Recharge Plate suspended over the drop. Fly to the middle height of the tall room, where two Red Orbs float cattycorner from each other on opposite sides of the room.

Drop to the ground and recharge your gauges after collecting orbs. Fly back up to the globe fixed in the center point of the machinery. Strike it repeatedly while in Devil Trigger, until all the white squares are converted to purple. A platform drops from the ceiling, and Puia materialize to attack. The vulture demons will materialize constantly until Lucia leaves the room, so at some point you'll have to stop fighting and move on.

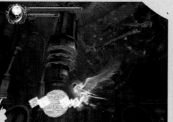

Use the God of Time statue near the mechanism if needed, and grab the **Green Orb** near the exit.

TARTUSSIAN

RECOMMENDED SWORD	CUTLASEER
RECOMMENDED ARSENAL	THROWING DAGGERS
RECOMMENDED AMULET	AERIAL HEART, FROST HEART

Move a short ways into the clock chamber to meet Lucia's first main opponent. Although Tartussian is itself a prisoner of the devils, this two-headed chain-swinging freak will give the protector quite a battle. Tartussian is weak against electric attacks, so Lucia won't be able to do severe damage until a replay game.

Tartussian's chains are connected to massive iron balls, which it flings and spins like a couple of toys. Tartussian throws these massive bearings with amazing precision, even knocking Lucia out of the sky if she is flying.

Leap around the edges of the room, and toss Throwing Daggers from midair until Lucia's Devil Trigger gauges fill. Keep tossing daggers until the monster becomes defensive, and swings one of its chains to deflect Lucia's projectiles. Then jump or Flip Escape behind Tartussian, Devil Trigger, and chain together several melee attacks. Try to spark a stylish combo, and continue it even after Lucia's power meter runs dry. Avoid standing in front of the monster, especially if Lucia is not in Devil Trigger.

Repeat this process until Lucia refills her Devil Trigger meter a bit, then run behind the monster and attack in Devil Trigger once again. Two such close range attacks should be enough to topple the gargantuan in your first game.

TOWER PEAK

Enter the small chamber revealed by the death of Tartussian, and approach the altar to add the Arcana Spada to Lucia's collection. The exit to the roof of the tower opens. Smash whatever gargoyle statues remain in the battle chamber to obtain Red Orbs, and then continue up to the rooftop.

To the left inside the altar room is a **Blue Orb Fragment**!

Move to the right around the backside of the bell tower to collect Red Orbs. Then move to the ledge and carefully Air Hike to a position directly above the Red Orbs hovering off the side of the building, so that Lucia can collect them as she drops to the mission end point.

MISSION COMPLETE!	
S RANK REQUIREMENTS	
CLEAR TIME	10:00 MINUTES
ORBS	2500
STYLISH AVERAGE	10 "SHOW TIME!!" COMBOS
DAMAGE	0
ITEM USED	NONE

MISSION 3

"In quiet desperation, the coastal town is hiding from the prowlers roaming the streets. The protector must collect the tools of justice and battle to the edge of the waters. High within the tower of light, the healing heart shall mend. For the protector needs protection as well, from the devil which would rend. She has many arms but only one heart, as she waits for the protector deep in the water."

-Guidepost for the Protectors *Chapter 4 Clause 5*

THE DEADLY STREETS

Head out of the alley and continue up the street beyond a Y-shaped intersection to a massive door at the end. Fend off sets of Agonofinis, then Kick Jump up to the top of two columns nearby for Red Orbs. Return to the Y-intersection and head down the street to the left.

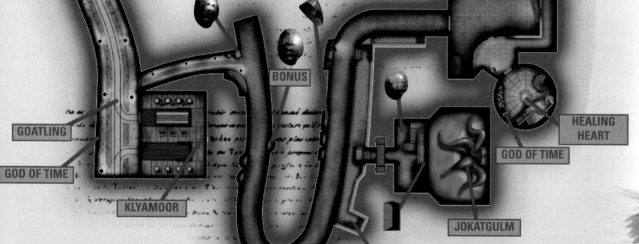

EXPLODING STREET

Move down the street until a red barrier seals off the area. A Goatling at the bottom of the street targets Lucia with spells that burst up from under her. Avoid being caught in a blast by running left or right when a black cloud appears under Lucia's feet. Ignore the enemies that appear, and zigzag down the street until Lucia is in close range of the Goatling. Once the horned enemy is defeated, all enemies on the street will disappear. Use the God of Time statue on the right side of the street if desired, and enter the brown door at the end on the left side of the street.

Double Red Orbs are stacked high above two lampposts at the top of the hill.

KLYAMOOR

Swords for Lucia that have wide range.

At the back of the trolley station are the **Kylamoor**. Lucia's new swords have extended range, but less attack power. Use the God of Time statue outside the station to improve their level if possible.

ROAD TO THE DOCKS

Exit the trolley station and move back up the street a few paces to a tall door with angel gates. Head down the narrow alley until a Red Orb is spotted overhead. Using the Aerial Heart to help if possible, fly up to grab the Red Orb, and land on the thin ledge. Kick Jump up to the next ledge higher up, and double jump from that ledge straight up to grab a whole **Blue Orb**.

Collect Red Orbs from the balcony across the gap as well as above the tall door at the end of the street

Descend the sloping street to encounter a large group of Msira. Jump up to a stone jut embedded in the left rock face, and move carefully around the ledge until Lucia triggers the release of many **Bonus Red Orbs**. Collect another Red Orb from the wall ruins on the opposite side of the street, and defeat the second set of Msira near the impassable seawall. Smash through the planks barring the doorway at the bottom of the street and continue down the hill to the seaport area.

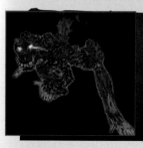

MSIRA

Msira are hunched and misshapen feral demons who lust for blood and chaos. They're more resilient than other types, and several strong sword attacks may be required to strike a stylish combo from one of them. Be prepared to Flip Escape out of the way, because Msira can leap long distances to swipe Dante with their claws.

SHIPPING ZONE

Proceed down the road until the lighthouse looms into view. Begin Kick Jumping up the cliff faces on the left, to reach a **Blue Orb Fragment** at the top.

Drop from the cliffs and jump along the rooftops of the low buildings on the left to snatch up more orbs. Work your way over to the doors of the lighthouse.

GEM OF LIFE

Defeat a set of Agonofinis inside the lighthouse to unseal the door on the level above. Check the large stone carving of Neptune under the stairs to find a Secret Room.

SECRET ROOM LOCATION 1

Stand below the engraving of Neptune below the stairs in the lobby of the light-house, and search this area to find a Secret Room.

Jump to the apex of the room to find a large Red Orb.

Lucia obtains the **Healing Heart** in the lighthouse mechanical room upstairs. While this stone is equipped in her Amulet, Lucia will regenerate vitality in her life meter while in Devil Trigger. Use the God of Time statue to the right if needed.

ENTRANCE OF THE SHE-DEVIL'S LAIR

Exit the lighthouse and proceed along the docks back toward the starting point. Head past the archway to the garage at the end, and abuse the Striking Stone until time runs out.

Return to the arch-way and follow a string of lit-tle Red Orbs onto the pier. Head left to grab a **Green Orb**, then enter the tall doors to face off against another of Arius's devils.

SECRET ROOM LOCATION 2

Before entering the boss fight, head up the stairs to the left of the door on the pier, move all the way across the parapet and search the area the end to find a Secret Room.

JOKATGULM

RECOMMENDED SWORD	CUTLASEER
RECOMMENDED ARSENAL	DARTS
RECOMMENDED AMULET	AERIAL HEART, FROST HEART, HEALING HEART

During a replay of the game, remember that Jokatgulm is weak versus fire, and that the Zambak swords are actually better to use.

Damage is only inflicted to Jokatgulm by attacking the central body stem, which is guarded by four tentacles. At least one of the tentacles must be eliminated to be able to attack the body at all. The tentacle will respawn in roughly 10 seconds, so that doesn't leave much time to inflict damage. If you're standing inside the tentacles when all four are active, the Jokatgulm will erect a shield, knocking Lucia away from the monster.

Severing tentacles is the main chore for most of the fight. Stay to one side of the creature, so that Lucia is dealing with only one or two tentacles instead of all four. Position her near the wall at the outside of the area, and leap over the limbs as they swing left or right. Fire volleys of Darts from the air, with the hopes of hitting the two closest tentacles at the same time.

When one or more tentacles are destroyed, double jump and Devil Trigger. Fly at the creature and begin striking the central body stem with hard sword attacks and kick combos. Unfortunately, Lucia will very likely suffer poisoning from the purple gas cloud that Jokatgulm spews in response. However, if you want to inflict a lot of damage quickly, this is unavoidable. When the tentacles you've severed reappear, try to leap away safely before the monster ejects Lucia forcefully. Resume flinging Darts at the tentacles until one disappears, then Devil Trigger and attack again. This strategy must be repeated several times to end the battle.

MISSION COMPLETE!

S RANK REQUIREMENTS

CLEAR TIME	8:00 MINUTES
ORBS	5000
STYLISH AVERAGE	20 "SHOW TIME!!" COMBOS
DAMAGE	0
ITEM USED	NONE

MISSION 4

"The city of evil is infested with corruption. Only one bear the heart of offense can surmount a city. Dodge flame tubes and navigate through the cracked city streets so that when the time comes, your path will be shown."

-Guidepost for the Protectors *Chapter 5 Clause 6*

DOOMED METROPOLIS

Head toward the low curved wall surrounding the tunnel entrance, and move along the wall until the camera angle includes a **Blue Orb Fragment** suspended at the apex of the curve. Jump for it carefully, or Devil Trigger and use the Aerial Heart to fly to it if you can.

Remember the God of Time statue located on the west side of the area, if you gain enough orbs to use it.

Landing below, Lucia must defeat a large set of hideous ectoplasm enemies called Infestants. Each is hard to kill, so use your hard-hitting martial arts kicks to strike stylish combos off each. When the set is defeated, the seal on a nearby altar is released. Approach the altar to receive the **Offence Heart**. Lucia hits much harder in Devil Trigger mode, when this stone is equipped on the Amulet.

INFESTED TANK

ORANGGUERRA

OFFENCE HEART

START

INFESTANT

These are the true forms of the gossamer creatures capable of fusing with military vehicles and other machines, bringing them alive unnaturally. Infestants are tough creatures, mostly because they barely exist in the real world until they have fused with an object. When the opportunity arises, they will attempt to take over the characters' bodies, draining a severe amount of vitality until shrugged off. If tackled by an Infestant, wiggle the left stick and roll your thumb over the face buttons of the controller to be set free more quickly. The character can break free instantly by entering Devil Trigger. Launch Throwing Daggers at an Infestant from a distance, until Lucia is close enough to do some real damage with her kicks.

ORANGGUERRA

You may have to defeat another set of Infestants while making your way out of the subterranean tunnel. Reachin the end of the ramp, Lucia encounters an overgrown ape with the ability to fire large force balls across long distances. Us Devil Trigger to help you eradicate this monster, and snuff out the Puia circling in the skies overhead. The barriers are removed from around the area when all the monsters are defeated. Head toward the breadcrumb path of small Red Orbs that lead to a tunnel in the northwest corner.

INFESTED TANK

RECOMMENDED SWORD	CUTLASEER
RECOMMENDED ARSENAL	THROWING DAGGERS
RECOMMENDED AMULET	AERIAL HEART, FROST HEART, OFFENSE HEART

The Infestants have found a suitable host, and brought an armored military tank to life! This battle can be easily won by using the environment to your advantage. Leap onto the side ledges or the bridge crossing the sunken street, and pelt the Infested Tank with Throwing Daggers until it dies. Positioning Lucia on the sidewalk directly to the left or right of the tank is most advantageous, so that you might be able to see the turret turn and the cannon nozzle pointed directly at your character and jump out of the way if needed.

The battle ends a little more quickly if you leap back and forth over the tank, tapping ⭘ like crazy to toss daggers in rapid hand over hand style. Avoid landing on top of the turret, because a small machinegun mounted near the hatch will blast Lucia off the top. This should be an easy battle where you can make a high Boss Clear Bonus.

MISSION COMPLETE!	
S RANK REQUIREMENTS	
CLEAR TIME	5:30 MINUTES
ORBS	1600
STYLISH AVERAGE	20 "SHOW TIME!!" COMBOS
DAMAGE	0
ITEM USED	NONE

MISSION 5

"Evil's heart receives its power from the source. The source must be rooted out and exploited so that the hunter may accomplish his task. The protector must rise to confront destiny head-on."

-Guidepost for the Protectors *Chapter 7 Clause 1*

STRIKING GLOBE

DEVIL TRIGGER RECHARGE PLATE

START

EVIL HEART

GOD OF TIME

CRANKY BOMBS

FLAME HEART

DEVIL TRIGGER RECHARGE PLATE

STRIKING GLOBE

ELECTRO HEART

INVESTIGATE THE POWER PLANT

Proceed out of the nook that houses the entrance of the power plant, and head all the way across the raised area to gather the Red Orb in front of the shutter door. No power is supplied, so the shutter cannot be opened. Restoring the power is Lucia's first objective.

Drop to the sunken level and defeat a small horde of Msira and Homromsira. Lucia's frost attacks in Devil Trigger are frighteningly effective against the flaming varieties. Clearing the area, jump up the catwalks on the far side of the area to reach the door at the top, which is highlighted by the placement of Red Orbs.

Run through the corridor and the following door to enter a large airplane hangar. Defeat Puia and Agonofinis surrounding a large cargo plane, then a second set of the stronger Terreofinis. Enter the open cargo ramp at the rear of the freighter.

Jump up while passing through the doorway in the corridor to find a large hidden Red Orb.

TERREOFINIS

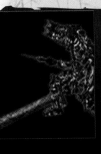

Hopefully you've been improving the strength of your weapons, because the tougher and more sinister brothers of the Agonofinis just showed up. Most are armed with the same type of weapons, and unarmed Terreofinis are going to attempt their "possession" attack more often. Don't let the devil hunter get sucked inside those cages. Like other metal-encased foes, Terreofinis are weak versus electric attacks.

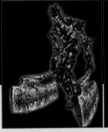

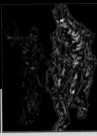

CRANKY BOMBS

Inside the cargo plane, smash the cargo box on the right side to obtain the **Cranky Bombs**. These are extremely powerful explosive charges that Lucia will toss at enemies, but they can also be tricky to use. When Lucia is standing still, she will drop the bomb at her own feet and slide backward. When a Cranky Bomb is thrown while pressing the Left Analog Stick, Lucia will hurl it for a certain distance. You must get used to the two distances and the timing of throwing these weapons before they can be adequately utilized. Cranky Bombs are Lucia's best weapon against large enemies such as goat-types.

POWERING THE PLANT

Exit the cargo plane and continue to the door at the back of the hangar. Use the Devil Trigger Recharge Plate to fill those gauges, and strike the globe in the center the small room until it activates.

With power restored to the facility, the massive fan at the top of the hangar begins to rotate. The force of the intake will suck Lucia toward the top end. Allow the draft to pull you as you fight another enemy set and head back for the door in the opposite corner of the hangar.

Return to the starting point and fight another set of Msira and Homromsira if desired. Jump up to the large shutter door, which now has power and can be opened.

CURSED BY EVIL

Stepping into the outdoor courtyard area between buildings, a gem flies out of the sky and burrows into Lucia's torso. Although the **Evil Heart** will gradually reduce Lucia's health until nothing remains, it cannot kill her. However, if the vitality bar is empty, the next enemy attack will kill her. You must rid yourself of this cursed item quickly! Equip the Healing Heart in the Amulet, so that Lucia can regain health by Devil Triggering occasionally.

While slowly working your way to the door at the bottom of the courtyard, take out Puia with the Throwing Daggers. Don't miss a string of little Red Orbs in one of the lower sections.

Double-jump from the top stair and fly across the area to the top of the curly pipes, where a **Gold Orb** remains hidden from normal view.

Tall silos on the left side of the area encircle a **Blue Orb Fragment**.

SPIRAL DESCENT

Strike the globe just inside the doorway until it activates. A protective shield around a gemstone at the top of the central area is removed.

The trip down the stairs to the bottom level is a time-consuming trip, and Lucia could lose a lot of health in the process. Plus, enemy sets of Homromsira and Spiceres arrive to complicate matters. But if you've managed to store up a full line of Devil Trigger power, you can make the descent more swiftly and recharge Lucia's vitality gauge in the process.

Run past the enemies, who would be destroyed by the Spiceres anyhow, and keep running until you reach the bottom.

111

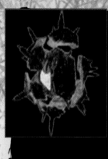

SPICERE

Luckily these floating orbs of self-destructing death will be rarely encountered, because they detonate when Dante is in the proximity or when they're fired upon. Any other enemy types in range of the blast are destroyed, without releasing any Red Orbs. Whenever Spiceres are encountered in enemy groups, the best you can hope for is to annihilate the whole group by destroying the Spicere, and that Dante won't get caught in the blast.

Although a Red Orb stands in front of a greenish-lit door, ignore it for the moment and continue around the silo. At the end of the path is a Devil Trigger Recharge Plate, so that Lucia can regain all that she just used. If you had to take the slow descent, recharge your gauges, Devil Trigger until her vitality is full, and recharge your gauges again.

Enter the bottom doorway into the center of the column, and attack the Striking Stone until it yields orbs no more. Fly up through the center until Lucia reaches the ceiling, then land on the platform and move to collect the **Flame Heart**. Lucia can now use the fire element in all her Devil Trigger attacks.

END OF THE CURSE

Enter the greenish-lit door near the bottom of the spiral stairs. Using the God of Time statue at the bottom of the stairs in the next room pauses the debilitating effects of the Evil Heart. Jump into the pit and follow the Red Orb into the middle doorway.

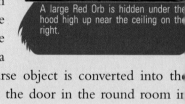

Cross directly through the rounded room and into the small nook. Touching the plate at the back of this area, Lucia inserts the Evil Heart. The curse object is converted into the **Electro Heart**. Head through the door in the round room in which a blue gem is embedded.

A large Red Orb is hidden under the hood high up near the ceiling on the right.

RED RAILS

Move along the rails until a dangerous group of Blood Goats appears. The rails can be used as obstacles to slow down these tougher members of the goat demon clan. Simply jump to the opposite side of the rails, and the horned demons can be saturated with Darts or blown up with Cranky Bombs while Lucia stands safe for the moment on the other side. Equip the Flame Heart in the Amulet and use Devil Trigger to get out of any tough spots.

BLOOD GOAT

A taller, stronger and more resilient version of Goatlings, these evil ceremonial monsters can remain in the air longer, and won't hesitate to pelt devil hunters with multiple homing missiles. The same tactics used to defeat their weaker siblings also work for this type, but it's a good idea to weaken them up a little with gunfire before attempting to knock them flat with sword attacks.

Grab the two Red Orbs at the end of the second tunnel and then run to the end of the rails. Smash the crates stacked to the left of the lift platform to gain more orbs. Hop onto the crate and Kick Jump up to a small ledge high on the wall. Devil Trigger and fly across the top of the area, collecting two more large Red Orbs.

A LIFT UP

Jump onto the lift to trigger Lucia's ascent. Battle Flambats as the platform rises. Continue to eliminate them as the elevator arrives at the top floor.

Entering the door in the center of the back wall ends the mission. First, smash the crates and barrels to obtain orbs, and check the door on the right to enter a Secret Room.

SECRET ROOM LOCATION 1

Before touching the door that ends the mission, check the door at the top of the steps on the right to find a Secret Room.

MISSION COMPLETE!	
S RANK REQUIREMENTS	
CLEAR TIME	7:30 MINUTES
ORBS	3000
STYLISH AVERAGE	20 "SHOW TIME!!" COMBOS
DAMAGE	0
ITEM USED	NONE

"The protector, the king, and the truth. Distracted by betrayal, the protector must overcome the soul denizen of the other world. The path to the deep water temple will be revealed."

-Guidepost for the Protectors *Chapter 7 Clause 1*

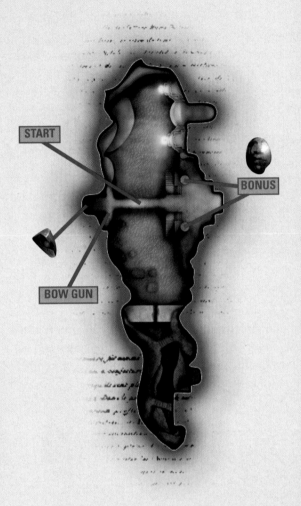

START

BONUS

BOW GUN

CONFRONTING ARIUS

Lucia is teleported to an alternative dimension. Defeat two Savage Golems to initiate a boss fight that is extremely difficult for Lucia. There will be plenty of Demonochorus in the air as well, so be sure to take them all out before killing the second Savage Golem. Build up your Devil Trigger gauges as much as possible with strong martial arts combos, because you're going to need it!

DEMONOCHORUS

Do not mistake these tiny flying orphans for cherubs, because their intentions are hardly noble. Jump into the air to target them, and use a volley of strong gunfire to bring them to the ground. Once a Demonochorus hits the dirt, quickly smash them to bits with hard sword attacks. Due to the hard metal shells in which these evil spirits are encased, they are quite resilient to firearms. However, to render them asunder with a blade, they must be brought to earth somehow. Demonochorus allowed to remain airborne too long will target Dante, in the form of a glowing halo that surrounds him. Quickly leap out of the way to avoid the resulting explosion.

NOCTPTERAN, LARVA

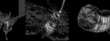 

RECOMMENDED SWORD	CUTLASEER
RECOMMENDED ARSENAL	THROWING DAGGERS, DARTS
RECOMMENDED AMULET	AERIAL HEART, FLAME HEART, HEALING HEART

The flying moth gives birth to an endless supply of Larva, and so it must be eliminated first. Air Hike (⊗ ⊗) high in the air directly beneath it, and when Lucia targets Noctpteran hold **R1** to lock on. Don't relinquish your lock on until this devil is buried in the dirt. Do not remain on the ground more than an instant, or a Larva might gulp her down. Jump up and saturate the flyer with Throwing Daggers, until the Devil Trigger gauges are full. With the Aerial Heart equipped, fly up to the Noctpteran's level and blast it with rapid-fire flame attacks until the creature falls to the ground.

Although the Noctpteran is done for, it will eject several more Larva from its tail section before evaporating. Run to the rear side of the monster, equip the Cranky Bombs and blast the newborn before they can escape into the earth. If you can prevent a few of these from burrowing, then there will be less to deal with for the rest of the battle.

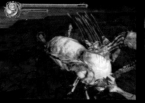 

Full-grown Larva erupt through the surface and chase after Lucia. The surface is a dangerous place, especially while two or more Larvae are still active. Every time Lucia lands, jump immediately. If it looks like she's about to fall directly into a Larva's mouth, press ⊗ again to Air Hike away. Use the Darts to blast their hides, and make wise use of the Green Orbs at the four corners of the area.

If a Larva swallows Lucia, rapidly wiggle the Left Analog Stick and roll your thumb over the face buttons of the controller to get free. Although she takes severe damage, Lucia frees herself from the Larva by exploding out of it! This is also a valid way to defeat the Larva and end the battle, but at some cost of vitality. Following the death of the last Larva, a portal to the normal world shall appear.

CAVERNS OF DESPAIR

Lucia is teleported to an underground cavern above a small lake. From her starting position, turn around and head into the arches on the back wall, to obtain two large Red Orbs and a **Blue Orb Fragment**.

Head back across the narrow bridge toward the all-seeing eye on the opposite side of the cavern. Use Devil Trigger to fly up to the top of the two columns on either side of the bridge's edge, and land on top each to release two clouds of **Bonus Red Orbs**.

Drop into the waters directly below the slender bridge, and swim into a small blue-lit nook to find the **Bow Gun**. This is an extremely fast and powerful weapon, for use only underwater but limited in range.

SWIMMING LESSONS

Swimming is very much like flying, but through water. Move the left stick to swim. Lucia will gradually sink in the water while swimming. Hold ○ to descend more swiftly. Tap ○ rapidly if you want to dive faster. To rise while swimming, hold ⊗ while moving the left stick. Tap ⊗ rapidly if you wish to rise sooner.

UNDERWATER COMBAT

Upon diving into the water, the Cranky Bombs will be equipped automatically. This is because the Cranky Bombs and the Bow Gun can be used underwater, whereas the others cannot. Lucia can also use any of her swords, but her slower underwater movement places her at a disadvantage against aquatic demons. The safest method to attack enemies is by dropping Cranky Bombs in depth-charge fashion, or by shooting them with the Bow Gun.

GUARDED DEPTHS

Swimming toward the exit under the red light, a school of Erupt Gels should materialize and attack. These are extremely tricky monsters that you'll want to attack only from a distance. Eliminate all the Erupt Gels and swim toward the door at the back of the tunnel to complete the mission.

ERUPT GEL

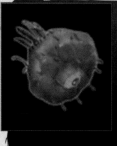

Erupt Gels resemble jellyfish in appearance. Although their eyes are large, they can only see a short distance. Erupt Gels are generally not fast swimmers, and they are usually not aggressive. They will attack only at extremely close range. However, when destroyed an Erupt Gel will burst into four small swimmers that move extremely fast. On contact with their target, they will explode into poisonous gas clouds. Lucia can suffer damage and poisoning from contact with the tiny offspring. After killing an Erupt Gel from a medium distance with the Bow Gun or Cranky Bombs, swim away from the little offspring and they will self-destruct harmlessly before long. The offspring can also be targeted and destroyed as a group with a Cranky Bomb.

MISSION COMPLETE!	
S RANK REQUIREMENTS	
CLEAR TIME	10:30 MINUTES
ORBS	2000
STYLISH AVERAGE	15 "SHOW TIME!!" COMBOS
DAMAGE	0
ITEM USED	NONE

MISSION 7

"Deep within the earth, the protector must find the strength to swim against the current. Rising above complications, only then can she send down the walls. Such actions may awaken that which was forgotten in the murky depths. Holy and filthy at the same time, some mysteries should be extinguished."

-Guidepost for the Protectors *Chapter 9 Clause 2*

BETWEEN MISSIONS: IMPROVE BOW GUN

Do yourself a huge favor and access the Power Up screen between missions. The Bow Gun is incredibly easy to improve, since only 4000 Red Orbs are required to reach Level 2 and only 8000 more to reach Level 3. With the Bow Gun at max level, Lucia should have no problems completing her underwater missions. Otherwise…

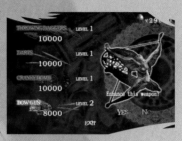

BLACK TIDE RISING

Swim forward along the left wall until Lucia finds an elusive cranny in which a cloud of **Bonus Red Orbs** is released. Glide under the vertical tunnel to the end of the initial passage, and nudge Lucia against the other wall until she finds a niche containing a whole **Blue Orb**. Finally, follow a string of small Red Orbs upward into a vertical tunnel.

STRIKING GLOBE

AQUA HEART

BONUS

GOD OF TIME

TATEOBESU

Tap ✕ rapidly to ascend all the way up the tunnel. Leaping out of the water into a small cave, Lucia will be automatically equipped with the Cranky Bombs. Press L2 until she is equipped with Throwing Daggers or Darts.

GEMSTONE OF THE DEPTHS

Drop from the entrance ledge and run through the shallow water to the platform on the other side. Lucia obtains the **Aqua Heart**, which enables speedy swimming underwater while in Devil Trigger.

After dispatching a group of Auromancers, smash the pots behind the altar and the ones beside the right hand door for orbs. The top of the altar is actually a ledge, from where you can leap up to another ledge on the left. Smash the pot on this ledge for a Red Orb, and check the archway engraving to find a Secret Room. Jump from there up to the highest ledge directly above the altar. Move into a small cave and smash all the pots for a quantity of Red Orbs.

SECRET ROOM LOCATION 1

Jump from the stone slab above the altar to the ledge on the right, and check the engraved archway to find a Secret Room.

AUROMANCER

Although no tougher in stamina or self-defense than Pyromancers, these hooded wizards cast a spell which fires icy homing missiles at Dante. For this reason alone, they provide a greater threat to the devil hunter than their flame-throwing siblings.

Drop to the ground and follow a string of Red Orbs through the right passage into a pit full of water. The tunnel emerges into a room where an overpowering current repels Lucia away from a pit in the floor. Ascend and enter the vertical tunnel above, to find machinery which will help cut off the current.

The rounded chamber above is filled with Sargassos. To activate the globes surrounding the room, the ghostly skulls must first be eliminated. A Sargasso will not activate until Lucia swims very close to it. The creature solidifies and attacks when your character is in close range. The best strategy for fighting them underwater is to swim past them, avoiding their initial attack. Swim behind the skull and attack with the Klyamoors.

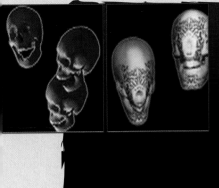

SARGASSO

Phantom skulls from the demon world, these avatars of doom are posted to stand vigilant in key locations so that the other demons may roam and prey. Sargassos appear in two varieties: the more regular skull-shaped type and also the brightly painted large kind. Sargassos remain spectral and cannot be damaged until your character is in extremely close proximity to them. Once they materialize, they will swoop in to attack quite swiftly. The best strategy is to move close to them, then jump away and pulverize them with the Shotgun.

Once the Sargassos are destroyed, Lucia must activate all the globes surrounding the room. Start at any globe, and press △ once to strike it. The next globe is always higher or lower than the last, so swim around the circular chamber and tap ✕ or ○ rapidly to surface or dive. If you sail past globes or take too long to strike them all, the initial globes eventually deactivate. Don't worry about starting over, just keep swimming around the circle and striking globes until a series of blue platforms appear above the water's surface.

Swim to the square platform floating on the surface, face it and tap ✕ to leap out of the water onto it. Perform Air Hikes from level to level around the center column. Jump onto the middle column and strike the globe object on top of the pillar.

Activating the globe object on top of the column lowers a wall in the large room one level below, where the current was too strong. Swim back down the vertical tunnel and descend through the square room into the rounded pit below. Tapping the ○ button has no real effect on diving, but Lucia can be made to swim downward faster if you rotate the Left Analog Stick to swim in circles while holding ○.

Use the God of Time statue to power up the Bow Gun or Cranky Bombs if possible. Collect the **Green Orbs** on either side of the icon and swim through the door.

TATEOBESU

RECOMMENDED SWORD	KYLAMOOR
RECOMMENDED ARSENAL	BOW GUN, CRANKY BOMBS
RECOMMENDED AMULET	AQUA HEART, FLAME HEART, OFFENCE HEAR

Ready for a test of your swimming abilities? The trick to outmaneuvering Tateobesu is to hold ✖ while moving Lucia with the Left Analog Stick. This way, she will maintain her current depth without sinking further. Allowing Lucia to drop to the bottom makes her an easy target. When Tateobesu charges in for an attack, tap ✖ rapidly as you swim to the left or right of the creature. If Lucia is already at ceiling height, press ⬤ and swim to the side of the monster to descend.

Tateobesu has two attacks. While swimming invisible in stealth mode, the monster attempts to position itself near Lucia and electrify the surrounding water. If Lucia swims to the rear of the camouflaged monster, its tail

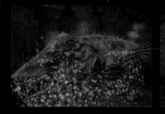 

swishes back and forth attempting to slap her. When the creature enters stealth mode, it's important to avoid disturbances and currents in the water that might be the big fish. Since the creature cannot be locked onto while invisible, the only way to damage it in this way is to swim above the creature and drop Cranky Bombs onto it. Since there's very little chance of blowing this fast-moving fish out of the water, utilize this tactic only during instances where Lucia has no Devil Trigger power remaining.

The other main attack begins when the creature becomes visible, opens its mouth and swims at Lucia with great speed. Break off attacking and swim to either side of the charging creature to escape its massive jaws. While Tateobesu glides past Lucia, lock on with the Bow Gun and fire several volleys into its sides. This is the best and only method to cause damage and raise the Devil Trigger gauges. Attempts to inflict melee damage are mostly damaging to Lucia. Swim and shoot, and avoid the monster.

To force Tateobesu to become visible and inflict the most damage possible during this battle, equip the Aqua Heart and Devil Trigger. Transformed Lucia can inflict damage whether Tateobesu is visible or not. Equip the Offence Heart to increase the damage of her Devil Trigger attacks, since this is the only real way to fight the ancient sea beast. Also, if you have a little Devil Trigger power and you can't seem to shake off the monster, use a short burst of Devil Trigger to swim away at incredible speeds.

When Tateobesu goes belly up, swim up through the opening in the ceiling to complete the mission.

MISSION COMPLETE!

S RANK REQUIREMENTS

CLEAR TIME	7:00 MINUTES
ORBS	4000
STYLISH AVERAGE	10 "SHOW TIME!!" COMBOS
DAMAGE	0
ITEM USED	NONE

MISSION 8

"The protector's path to the final piece is a submerged den of murk and corruption. Rising above the waters, the fire of the gods must be used against them. Out of the abyss, the protector must rise to obtain the ceremonial object. Defeat the prisoner in the abyss and hand the hunter the mysterious vessel."

-Guidepost for the Protectors *Chapter 9 Clause 9*

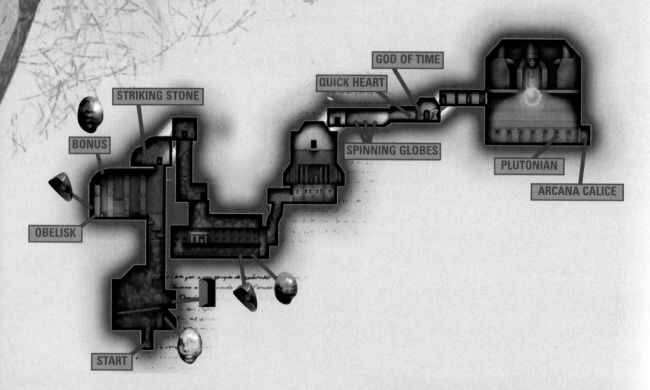

ENTER THE BLADES

Swim up out of the square pit to encounter a much tougher breed of underwater foes: the Blades. Shoot these creatures from medium range with the Bow Gun until they begin to thrash in the water, then close in and slash them apart with the Kylamoors. There are many secrets hidden in this single chamber, so you may have to deal with multiple respawning sets of Blades and Erupt Gels until you find everything and swim up to the water's surface.

A **Gold Orb** is tucked behind a fallen slab under the ledge, below a doorway where a large Red Orb floats.

Swim into this dark "doorway" and search the back wall to find the entrance of a Secret Room.

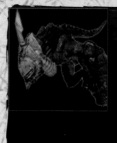

BLADE

Propelling itself through the water with webbed feet, this aquatic lizardman can charge at Lucia like a torpedo. From a distance, the Blade will fire sharp little scales that penetrate Lucia like bullets. Shoot with the Bow Gun to distract them, then swim in and attack with Lucia's swords.

TRIAL BY FIREBALL

Glide around the circular area to collect the little Red Orbs. Then swim under the ledge on the lower left side of the circular opening, and tap ✗ rapidly to surface. When Lucia leaps out of the water, hit ✗ again to double jump and land on the stone ledge. Leap out of the circular pit onto the surrounding ground.

Move behind the large obelisk at the other end of the room, to find a hidden **Blue Orb Fragment**. Check the front of the object to enter a true challenge of your timing skills.

The obelisk will begin to launch fireballs on a horizontal trajectory straight across the room, so leap out of the way after initializing this event. Stand near the wall of the circular pit. Each fireball is preempted by a glow around the eye painted on the obelisk. After each fireball is launched, it takes exactly one second to reach Lucia's position at the edge of the circular pit. So when the fireball launch sound occurs, count in your head "One thousand one". Then press △ to hit the fireball and knock it back at the obelisk. If Lucia misses, she will suffer a minor amount of damage, which unfortunately is counted against your damage ranking for the mission. You must knock three fireballs back at the obelisk in order to destroy it.

Reflect my power...

The room is flooded instantly with water and Erupt Gels. This enemy set will respawn faster than you can kill them so leave the room after eliminating just a few of them.

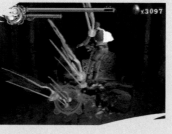

Swim up into the light hole above the destroyed obelisk to discover Bonus **Red Orbs**.

UNDERWATER CATACOMBS

Leap through the hole in the ceiling onto dry land once again. Attack the Striking Stone until it runs dry on orbs, and then smash a pot in the nook on the wall for another big red one. Head through the corridor and jump to the center of the pit to grab the Red Orb on the way down. Swim to the bottom of the chamber and through the doorway.

Descend through the rounded chamber and defeat a set of Blades and Erupt Gels. Collect the little Red Orbs on the two pedestals, and then descend through a square hole in the floor. Swim back through the narrow chamber to collect a **Green Orb**, a **Blue Orb Fragment**, and several large red Orbs. Swim either direction to the chamber above, and proceed through the twisting vertical tunnel to the next area.

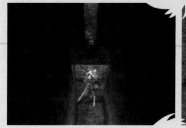

TRANSFORMING TILES PUZZLE

Jumping into a small corridor, run through the door and the next chamber to the opposite wall. Kick Jump up the wall to the blue sigil in the small niche. Examine the sigil to activate a tile on the floor below.

Touching the center tile activates a mechanism that raises and lowers tiles in the room, limiting access to four spinning globes. The objective is to destroy the glowing globes that appear. Each globe destroyed will change a flame on the back wall from red to blue. When all eight flames have been converted, a series of water platform will erupt from the floor so that Lucia can hop to freedom.

The situation is complex, because each set of globes will disappear after just a few seconds. Also, the floor tiles rise in various patterns and restrict access to the globes. As the globes disappear, the tiles will change formations. Jump over the rising tiles from globe to globe. Each time you press and release △, Lucia will perform two attacks. Attack each globe twice in this fashion to destroy it efficiently, then Air Hike across the raised tiles to the next globe.

The translucent water platforms can be tricky at first, but you can navigate them quickly and easily by single jumping from level to level, diagonally in some cases. Perform an Air Hike to reach the door at the top.

SPEED REWARDED FOR SPEED

Emerge from the narrow corridor and defeat a small set of poisonous Gbusmsira. Proceed into the next room to better understand your objective. An Amulet Stone is encased in a force field. To remove the barrier, Lucia must destroy all three spinning globes in the previous corridor, then dash into the second room and touch the unprotected gem before the globes reappear.

GBUSMSIRA

These monsters are a stronger variation of Msira, with higher levels of vitality. Their veins are filled with venom, and they can spit a substance that inflicts poison status for several moments. Their regular attacks, such as claw swipes and tackles, can cause poisoning as well. Keep your distance from them while shooting, and strike with the sword to spark stylish combos only when they are off-balance or staggering.

Equip the Aqua Heart, so that when you Devil Trigger, Lucia does not start flying by accident. To keep Lucia from sailing past each globe as she attacks, you must restrict her attacks. Tap △ slowly, so that she performs a kick and a chop, then settles. With the right timing, you can perform these two attacks repeatedly, and she will destroy each globe more efficiently with fewer wasted moves.

Each globe requires roughly ten of these attacks to destroy. Therefore, attack the globe closest to the gemstone eight times, and repeat with the middle globe. Now attack the third globe furthest from the Amulet stone until it breaks, and quickly destroy the two globes previously weakened up. When the blue shield drops, Devil Trigger and dash into the next room. Avoid bumping into the large crystal obstacles, and touch the altar to receive the **Quick Heart**.

Be careful not to enter the door at the end without smashing the stone coffins to the left and right.

Grab the **Green Orb** in the corner and use the God of Time statue to improve weapons or buy orbs to increase your meters. Grab a large Red Orb opposite from the statue, and proceed into the next corridor. Destroy the standing sarcophagi in the alcoves to obtain Red Orbs.

PLUTONIAN

RECOMMENDED SWORD	CUTLASEER
RECOMMENDED ARSENAL	THROWING DAGGERS
RECOMMENDED AMULET	QUICK HEART, ELECTRO HEART, OFFENCE HEART

Lucia fights another prisoner of the devils, assigned to protect the last Arcana. Much like the last two-headed chain boss, this one also whips around the two massive iron balls at the ends of his restraints and uses them as weapons to pulverize Lucia.

Throw daggers at Plutonian from a distance in order to raise your Devil Trigger gauges. Stay out of range of the iron balls, and use Air Hike (✕ ✕) or Flip Escape ◯ to avoid his long throws. When the Devil Trigger gauge is full, transform and run behind Plutonian. Attack his backside with electrically charged sword attacks. Watch the DT meters carefully as you strike and leap away when the power level drops to nil. Retreat and recharge the Devil Trigger gauges by attacking from a distance. Plutonian should topple easily after just a few more Devil Trigger assaults.

The environment complicates the battle by firing laser beams across the room. A beam is about to fire when a faint blue beam of light stretches across the room, and soon begins to grow brighter. Jump or Flip Escape away from the beams as they are forming. Since the beams start at one side of the room and progress to the other, you should escape in the direction where the beams have already shot. After the beams fire across the width of the room, they will begin shoot across the length of the chamber as well. When Plutonian's vitality is reduced to a fraction, both sets of beams will be firing simultaneously to create a net of lasers across the ground. Air Hiking very high into the air is then the only way to avoid the beams.

Keep in mind when playing through the next difficulty level that Plutonian's armor is sliced more easily with the thick Zambak blades.

FINAL ARCANA

Once Lucia has toppled another two-headed chain swinger, collect his Red Orbs and move toward the altar to obtain the **Arcana Calice**.

MISSION COMPLETE!	
S RANK REQUIREMENTS	
CLEAR TIME	8:30 MINUTES
ORBS	5000
STYLISH AVERAGE	20 "SHOW TIME!!" COMBOS
DAMAGE	0
ITEM USED	NONE

MISSION 9

"To prove its own identity, the protector points a blade toward the decayed king."

-Guidepost for the Protectors *Chapter 10 Clause 5*

ARIUS

RECOMMENDED SWORD	KYLAMOOR
RECOMMENDED ARSENAL	CRANKY BOMBS, THROWING DAGGERS
RECOMMENDED AMULET	QUICK HEART, FLAME HEART, HEALING

Arius is no match for the beautiful and skillful Lucia. The decrepit wizard attacks only with a pistol, and various dark spells such as Black Hole and Shadow Spikes. He can make himself invulnerable for brief periods merely by erecting a protective shell around himself, but it's only temporary. The main challenge of this battle is the monsters Arius calls upon to defend himself against Lucia's assault. As the battle progresses, the evil sorcerer will conjure tougher creatures such as Blood Goats, and only then could this battle become difficult. The key is to try to ignore the Jomothumsira who bodyguard their master, and target Arius himself with all of your attacks.

Leave Cranky Bombs under Jomothumsiras to blast them out of your path. Slash Arius with the Kylamoor swords, and build up Lucia's Devil Trigger gauges. If Arius teleports to a side of the room and sits idly on a desk, avoid battling any of the minor monsters and dash after the dark wizard, using Devil Trigger and the Quick Heart to move with blinding speed. Keep slashing away at Arius with strong sword attacks and Devil Trigger whenever the first line of your gauges is reached. Bash this bad guy with all the vengeance Lucia deserves, and then sit back for a few scenes.

MISSION COMPLETE!	
S RANK REQUIREMENTS	
CLEAR TIME	1:30 MINUTES
ORBS	1600
STYLISH AVERAGE	12 "SHOW TIME!!" COMBOS
DAMAGE	0
ITEM USED	NONE

MISSION 10

"Evil corrupts the soil and fills the air with an acidic taste. The protector must open a gateway to the foul one's lair by bringing illumination to the dark. Four lights will open the sealed door, but will also invite the creepy to play."

-Guidepost for the Protectors *Chapter 11 Clause 7*

VIDU MALI IN SHADOWS

To the left of Lucia's starting position is a God of Time statue. Remember its location throughout this mission, in case you want to improve weapons or extend Lucia's meters. Proceed forward through the large archway and check the first door on the left to find a Secret Room. Hop over the tall column tilting in from the right to get a Red Orb.

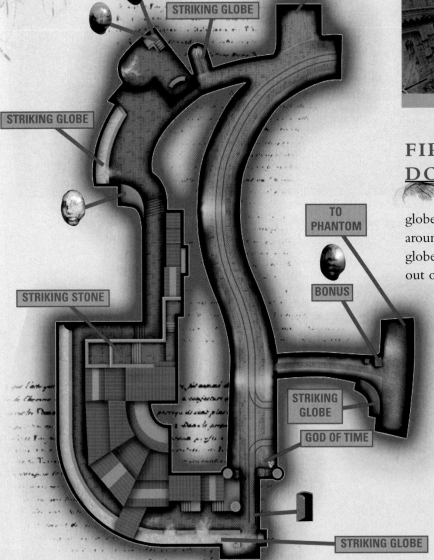

SECRET ROOM LOCATION 1

Moving forward from the starting point, check the first door on the left to find a Secret Room.

FIRST KEY TO THE DOORWAY

Head across the street and strike the blue globe on the corner until all the white squares around it turn purple. This is just one of four globes which must be activated to open a gateway out of this warped version of Lucia's hometown.

FLOATING FEROCITY

A trio of Abyss Goats will probably appear while Lucia is attacking the globe. While Dante's attacks against these aerial creatures are somewhat limited, Lucia can take them head on in midair with her Rapid Fire kick attack. Start this maneuver by Air Hiking into the sky in close range of an Abyss Goat. When Lucia is on the same level as the enemy, hold **R1** and move the left stick toward the enemy while tapping △.

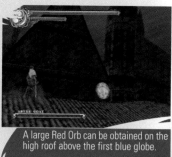

A large Red Orb can be obtained on the high roof above the first blue globe.

ABYSS GOAT

Kings among the goat-headed demons, the Abyss Goats are larger than the rest and have the sturdiest wings. Abyss Goats won't hesitate to take to the air and cast a deluge of magic missiles to track a target. A constant barrage of gunfire will eventually cause them to convulse in mid air, but they can remain aloft even after such an attack! Disrupt their aerial attacks by blasting them with the Missile Launcher. If an Abyss Goat does fall to the ground, chop them up really well using the Vendetta.

Jump over the low wall to face an incredibly large and difficult enemy set. Take out Blood Goats and Abyss Goats with Darts from the rooftop. Then drop to the ground to smash up some disc tossing Agonofinis. Avoid fighting in the street until the aerial foes are defeated. Getting caught between the two enemy types can be disastrous.

Smash a gargoyle statue in the corner near the turn in the long street to obtain two large Red Orbs.

TO THE SECOND GLOBE

Leap up to the parapets to utilize a Striking Stone for many Red Orbs. Head across the rooftops along the alleyway to find more orbs, then drop to the street and tangle with Gbusmsira and Jomothumsira. Beyond their zone, jump onto the ledge to the left to obtain a **Gold Orb**. Just around the corner is the second blue globe. Strike it until the device is activated.

JOMOTHUMSIRA

The toughest form of monkey-like demons, Jomothumsiras are almost impossible to knock off balance until their vitality is low, and their attacks are strong enough to knock even Dante off his feet! Use Shotgun blasts to keep them at bay, and try to eliminate groups with the Missile Launcher. Jomothumsiras are prime candidates to try the entire High Time move, with an uppercut, two mid-air kicks, followed by a hard chop to the ground. Tough monkeys deserve tough punishment!

MISSING AN AMULET STONE?

Jump through the opening high on the rounded corner. Defeat Jomothumsiras and Brontomancers in the deformed courtyard area. If Lucia failed to obtain the Quick Heart in the previous missions, an altar in this area will be unsealed when the first set of foes is defeated. Otherwise, this area is completely optional.

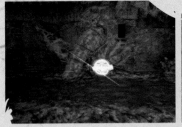

A complete **Blue Orb** and a **Green Orb** wait on the raised platform in the corner!

BRONTOMANCER

Appearing and disappearing to avoid harm, these spell-casting wizards are no stronger than their relatives but certainly are cleverer. Brontomancers cast lightning spells, which strike almost without warning, so whenever you see one of these enemies conjuring it's time to slash them into next week. Brontomancers attack and evade at higher rates than other dark spell casters.

TWO GLOBES DOWN...

Exit the courtyard and follow a string of Red Orbs through a narrow alley into the next area. Head right into a small alcove, and strike the blue globe until it activates.

SWORDS FOR BUTCHERY

Return to the street and continue forward all the way to the end, where two large Red Orbs stand. Fend off a large group of Savage Golems and Demonochorus, and move to the back of the side area to obtain the **Zambak** swords. These thick blades are excellent for cutting through the thick hides of armored or tall demons.

ACTIVATE THE FINAL GLOBE

Return to the Y-intersection and continue down the left path. Run down the street and dismantle a group of Agonofinis, starting with the disc wielding types. Keep going down the slope until Lucia returns to the starting point and then head down the alley to the left.

A large group of all the different types of spell casters appear at the bottom of the hill. Bait them into teleporting into the narrow area of the alley, so that they have less chance of surrounding Lucia.

When the large group of sorcerers is destroyed, Kick Jump up to the balcony where the large Red Orb floats. The next ledge higher up at the corner is impossible to reach by jumping. Equip the Aerial Heart, then Air Hike above the platform and Devil Trigger. Glide to a position above the top ledge and allow Lucia to descend and land. Move carefully around the ledge until a cloud of **Bonus Red Orbs** drops from the sky.

Flip over to the opposite ledge and strike the final blue globe until it activates. Then drop to the ground and follow a high line of little Red Orbs through the tall door.

THE GATEWAY

Entering this area after striking all four globes, four giant eyeballs surrounding the center will have been unsealed. A central eyeball rises through the sealed gateway. Move along the edge of the area to the left and Kick Jump high up to find a large Red Orb float-

ing near the wall. Although a **Green Orb** floats on the opposite side of the circular area, avoid using it unless really needed or during the boss fight. Move to the center and strike the central eyeball.

PHANTOM

RECOMMENDED SWORD	ZAMBAK
RECOMMENDED ARSENAL	THROWING DAGGERS
RECOMMENDED AMULET	AERIAL HEART, FROST HEART, OFFENCE HEART

Now it's time to see how Lucia's unique skills will fare against a classic devil such as the Phantom. While the Zambaks are the best swords to cut through the Phantom's skin of stone, use the Cutlaseers if they are at a higher level.

While the scorpion-like tail is extended, Air Hike high in the air directly above the Phantom and pelt it with dozens of Throwing Daggers. Stay airborne off the ground as much as possible to avoid letting the Phantom gain the upper hand. If the tail retracts and curls into a ball on the back of the Phantom, then land on top of the magma spider and toss daggers at its skull while standing right on top of it. What a cocky attack!

When Lucia's power gauges are full, Devil Trigger and dash right up to the unprotected face of the Phantom. Strike at the face as fast as possible with sword attacks, tinged with the cold power of the Frost Heart. Boosted by the Offence Heart, one barrage of attacks should be enough to reduce the Phantom's vitality meter to almost nothing.

If the Phantom becomes very still, even when Lucia is attacking at close range, it's time to escape. The Phantom summons geysers of lava to blast upward from the ground, preceded only by a little ruffle of dust on the ground. Use Flip Escape ⬤ to avoid magma columns, and don't worry about attacking until this attack stops occurring. The same is true for when the extended tail fires a meteor into the sky. Small but devastating meteorites will pelt the ground for several moments after this, but they can be avoided in the same fashion if you focus on dodging rather than attacking.

MISSION COMPLETE!	
S RANK REQUIREMENTS	
CLEAR TIME	7:30 MINUTES
ORBS	5500
STYLISH AVERAGE	20 "SHOW TIME!!" COMBOS
DAMAGE	0
ITEM USED	NONE

MISSION 11

"They swarm like clouds and desperately seek the protector's blood."

-Guidepost for the Protectors *Chapter 11 Clause 9*

Strike the eye in the center once more, to finally wrench open the demon gate. A timer appears onscreen, and enemies ambush Lucia. You must defeat a large double enemy set in less than three minutes, or the gateway closes again and the opportunity is lost. The first wave includes Jomothumsira and Demonochorus. The second wave consists mainly of Abyss Goats. The winged goat demons will quickly gang up on Lucia if you move too far across the area, so try to stay on one side of the center for most of the time. Let the enemies come to you, and use flame attacks in Devil Trigger to knock off the Abyss Goats. A Red Orb floats high on the right hand wall, and a **Green Orb** can be found at a tall level on the left. For Lucia, defeating the first set in the allotted time seems almost impossible.

Failure to defeat all the enemies before three minutes expires causes the gate to close and the enemies to dis-

appear. You've also lost your chance at an S ranking. Strike the central eye to try again. This time a much easier enemy set appears, and Lucia has four minutes to defeat them.

MISSION COMPLETE!	
S RANK REQUIREMENTS	
CLEAR TIME	3:30 MINUTES
ORBS	2000
STYLISH AVERAGE	8 "SHOW TIME!!" COMBOS
DAMAGE	0
ITEM USED	NONE

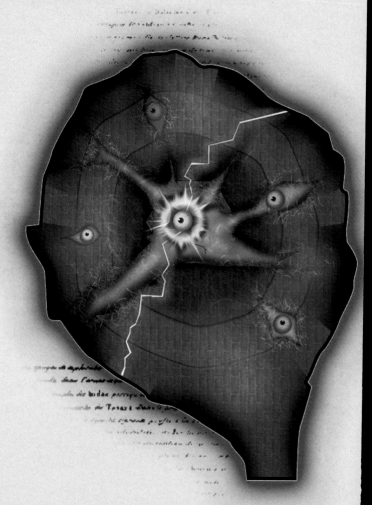

MISSION 12

"The Protector scales the skyscraper believing in its own reason for existence."

-Guidepost for the Protectors *Chapter 12 Clause 3*

GOAT FACTORY

The demon portal leads to the lobby of Arius' building. Approach the double doors, and they become sealed by the dark forces. Lucia must defeat several Blood Goats materializing in the lobby to unseal the elevator doors. Equip the Zambaks and the Flame Heart, and Devil Trigger whenever possible to help you win.

The Blood Goats have severe trouble attacking Lucia on the narrow stairs.

On the balcony above, move into the corner above and to the left of the elevator doors to find **Bonus Red Orbs**.

Just after the elevator doors close, the compartment is filled with Agonifinis and Terreofinis. Let those swords fly, and perform plenty of kicks in order to wrack up those high combo levels. Lucia will probably still be chopping up skeletons by the time the elevator reaches the top level, so exit at your leisure.

Head left from the elevator doors to the end of the corridor and smash the large vase to release a Red Orb. Check the wall behind the vase to find a Secret Room. Destroy the other two objects in the corridor for more orbs, and likewise with the rest of the destructible objects throughout the level.

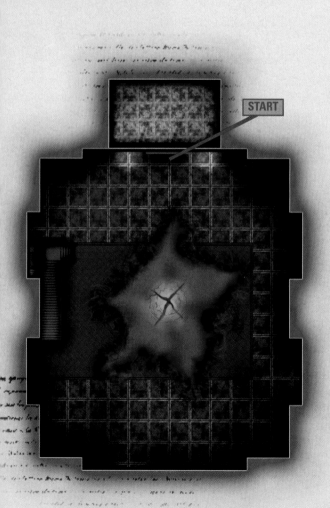

START

SECRET ROOM LOCATION 1

Move east from the elevator and destroy the vase at the end of the corridor. Check the center wall panel behind the vase to find a Secret Room.

ELEGANT CORRIDORS OF EVIL

Continue out of the corridor where the elevator stops to find a God of Time Statue. Against the wall to the right is a vase that can be smashed to obtain a **Green Orb**. Proceed through the next corridor, smashing more vases for Red Orbs and Air Hike up to the chandelier in the octagonal area for a big one.

SACRILEGIOUS MONKEYS

The third area on this level is a warped and twisted room. The face engraved on the door has an open mouth for a reason; it's hungry! Venture further into the room to find something to feed it.

The mouth is open leaving a space

Entering the tilted double-octagon area, Lucia is sealed inside the room until she can defeat a very large group of Jomothumsira. Don't hesitate to use Lucia's Devil Trigger to alleviate this large group. Run from one end of the room to the other if needed, just to avoid being surrounded. Use the **Green Orb** at the back of the room if required.

START

GOD OF TIME

SACRILEGE

When the last monkey demon bites it, a **Sacrilege** appears in the center of the room. Return with this item to the ugly face on the door, and the corridors will be rearranged to reveal a new area. Check your in-game maps to view the new layout and determine where the new area has appeared.

TRANSFORMING CORRIDOR

The connecting corridor now runs to a new area on the west side of the building. Destroy pots near all three doors to collect Red Orbs, and defeat small sets of mixed spell casting devils that materialize out of the blue to attack.

FURTHER BLASPHEMY

Enter the new area on the west side of the building, and proceed through the short corridor into the double-octagonal area. Another hungry mouth on the door needs to be fed, and the object of desire is held hostage by another ugly face on the top level at the end of the room.

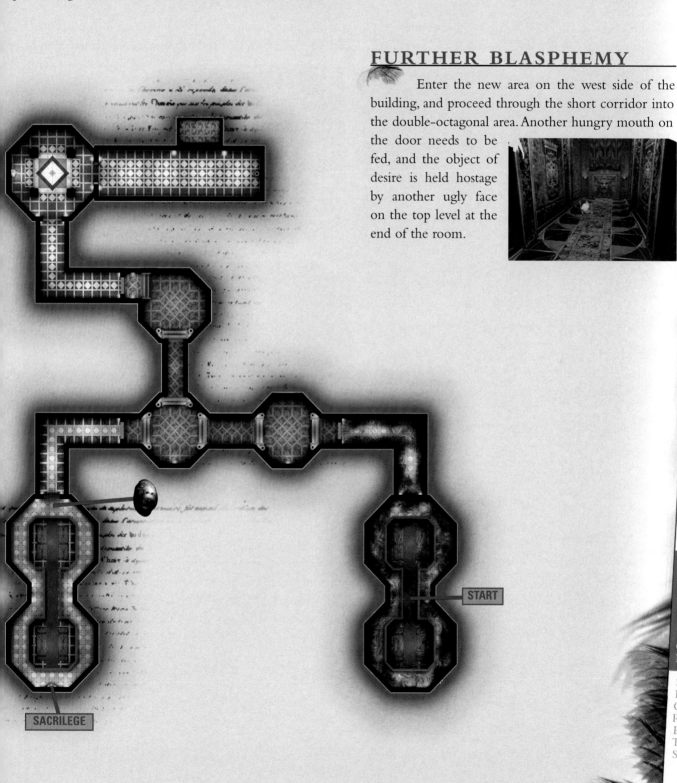

SACRILEGE

START

Crossing the area, translucent magic balls begin to fly across the length and width of the room. If one of these boulders strikes Lucia, she is transported to a violent alternative dimension where two Savage Golems must be eliminated in order for her to return to the real world. Unfortunately, teams of respawning Jomothumsira will do everything they can to distract the protector from striking the Savage Golems. Once you land an attack on one of the poisonous brutes, lock on and keep attacking until they are dead.

One of the easier ways to cross the room without bumping into a boulder is by Air Hiking to the upper level where the boulders are not so free to roll back and forth. Make your way around the outside of the area, and jump over boulders headed your way. When Lucia reaches the area surrounding the ugly face on the back wall of the room, the translucent balls stop rolling.

Be sure to collect Red Orbs from the side walls and corners of the balcony.

Don't miss the **Blue Orb** on the balcony just above the entrance to the double-octagon area.

Take the **Sacrilege** from one ugly face and return it to the other on the entrance. The connecting corridor between the rooms is changed around once again.

TWISTED GREEN

The corridor connecting all the areas becomes darker and more twisted than ever. Jomothumsira enemies appear in every wide area, so make a beeline for the new room that has appeared between the two lower areas on the map. A Red Orb guides you to the corridor running to the new area, and a **Green Orb** waits to replenish your vitality before entering.

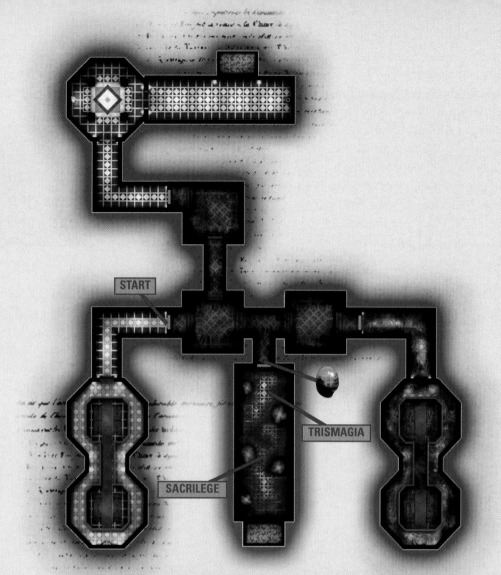

START

TRISMAGIA

SACRILEGE

TRISMAGIA

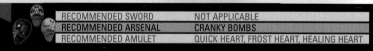

RECOMMENDED SWORD	NOT APPLICABLE
RECOMMENDED ARSENAL	CRANKY BOMBS
RECOMMENDED AMULET	QUICK HEART, FROST HEART, HEALING HEART

The first few seconds of the battle, there is nothing to do but wait for Trismagia to separate into three faces, representing the elements of electricity, frost and flame. Because the three colored faces take so little damage from any type of thrown weapon, it's more important to dodge attacks rather than trying to assault the enemy.

While the three faces are taking their turns to attack, work on building Lucia's Devil Trigger gauges. Allowing Lucia to get hit is one way to do it, because you can always regain lost vitality when the Healing Heart is equipped during Devil Trigger. Sometimes the frost face will launch five large icicles that crash into the floor and stick out of the ground. Bash your way through these columns with the swords to fill the DT gauges quickly.

After the three faces have all had a significant number of turns to attack, they will reform into a single creature. Now it's Lucia's turn! When the single head appears and becomes a target, Devil Trigger and hold the ⬤ button to blast the lone face with ice attacks. Trismagia will prepare a devastating combo beam attack while you fire. Move to one side of the platform to see the approaching blast with better visibility, and Flip Escape out of harm's way. When Trismagia separates again, hit L1 to turn off your Devil Trigger. Wait until the next time Trismagia unites, and perform the same attack again. Lucia must endure this routine through roughly three separations during a Normal difficulty game.

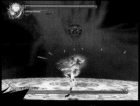
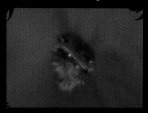

135

WHERE'S THE SACRILEGE?

Check to see how many Amulet Stones Lucia owns. If you have found all five, then simply proceed to the eleva-tor doors on the other side of the room and continue up to Arius' penthouse suite. But if Lucia has not obtained all five of the Amulet Stones by now, then you must force the fourth area on this level to appear. ***If you have all five Amulet stones, skip down to the section titled "Tough Ride".***

Trismagia leaves nothing behind for Lucia, but there's still a hungry face on the door to feed. Exit the room and immediately reenter. After defeating a group of Demonochorus and Abyss Goats in this ridiculously cramped space, the final Sacrilege appears in the center of the room. Use this on the door to rearrange the con-necting corridor and make a final area appear in the upper east corner of the map.

THE INTENSTINES OF HELL

The level is now divided into four squares outside the door to each area, with connecting corridors between each. Large groups of Mortfinis attack. Work your way to the new area in the upper east corner of the level.

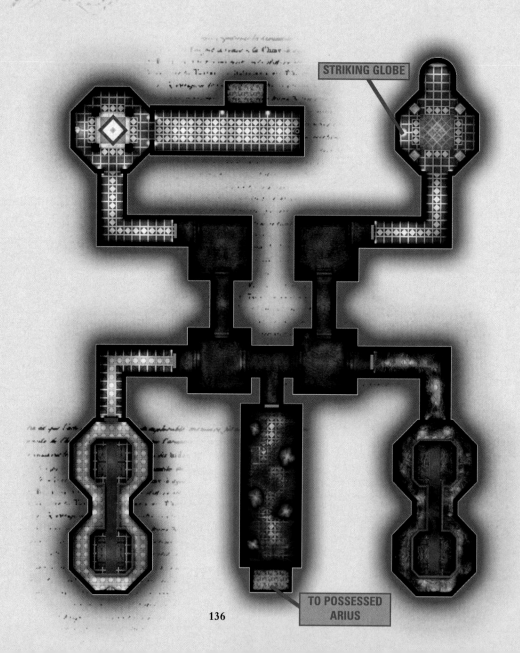

STRIKING GLOBE

TO POSSESSED ARIUS

MORTFINIS

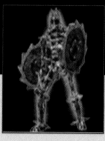

The last of the final form monsters, Mortfinis are slightly stronger in vitality and attack than Terreofinis and Agonofinis. If you've been leveling up your swords and weapons, they are still not a problem to deal with.

THE GOAT DEVIL CHAMBER

Four large petrified goat demons stand around the center of the main chamber, and a blue globe waits to be struck. When the globe object is activated, the four goat statues naturally come to life and attack. Lucia must defeat all four demons in order to obtain an Amulet Stone from the altar nearby.

Afterwards, return to the chamber where Lucia fought Trismagia. Cross to the elevator doors and enter.

TOUGH RIDE

Lucia's ascent to the penthouse suite is a rocky trip, hampered by a Blood Goat and scores of respawning Jomothumsiras. When the elevator arrives at the top level, do Lucia a favor and exit the car, rather than risk endless battles.

Grab a **Green Orb** in the corridor, then cross a short distance into the penthouse to end the mission.

MISSION COMPLETE!	
S RANK REQUIREMENTS	
CLEAR TIME	9:00 MINUTES
ORBS	7000
STYLISH AVERAGE	20 "SHOW TIME!!" COMBOS
DAMAGE	0
ITEM USED	NONE

MISSION 13

"The path to forgiveness is cleaned with blood."

-Guidepost for the Protectors *Chapter 13 Clause 1*

BEFORE THE MISSION: POWER UP!

If at all possible, purchase a Purple Orb before starting Mission 13. Not only will Lucia extend her Devil Trigger meter, but she also starts off at full power! This is a good way to get a head start on Arius.

POSSESSED ARIUS

RECOMMENDED SWORD	KYLAMOORS
RECOMMENDED ARSENAL	CRANKY BOMBS
RECOMMENDED AMULET	QUICK HEART, FLAME HEART, HEALING HEART

In life, Arius was a much less formidable opponent. But now that he is returned in a state of transmutation, he is the most dangerous opponent Lucia has faced yet.

Aside from all his melee attacks, Arius will submerge his tentacle arms under the earth. Unless Lucia is performing Flip Escapes like crazy, the tentacles will strike her for multiple hits of damage.
The other main attack to watch out for begins when Arius hovers off the ground. Unless Lucia can Devil Trigger and attack him immediately, Arius will fire a beam or spread of blasts which are sure to strike Lucia multiple times.

Circle around Arius and toss Cranky Bombs at him. While the blasts don't do a severe amount of damage, the Devil Trigger gauges will fill more quickly. Also, if Arius has launched two of his purple electric orbs that haunt Lucia wherever she goes, they will be destroyed by the blast. Dodge away from his attempted haymakers and other physical blows, and make wise use of the four **Green Orbs** situated in the corners of the area.

Lucia's main strategy for defeating Arius is much the same as the other bosses. When her Devil Trigger gauges are full, transform and run behind Arius. Attack him mainly with sword strokes, and leap away when Lucia's power meter empties. Roughly four such hyper-powered attacks plus a handy helping of Cranky Bombs between should easily finish this battle.

To obtain any amount of orbs from defeating his possessed form, you must finish off Arius while "Show Time!!" is onscreen, and you must be standing directly next to him in order to absorb the orbs.

ARIUS-ARGOSAX

RECOMMENDED SWORD	NOT APPLICABLE
RECOMMENDED ARSENAL	THROWING DAGGERS
RECOMMENDED AMULET	AERIAL HEART, FLAME HEART, HEALING HEART

Although Arius is bigger and nastier and has Lucia trapped in a deep chasm, this version is much easier to handle. Inundate it with Throwing Daggers as you move Lucia backwards. She should soon bump up against the end of the chasm. Keep flinging daggers at the head and avoid spews of poisonous vomit, until Lucia has one or two gauges filled in her Devil Trigger meter. Then transform and fly over the creature to its tail end. Run to the opposite end of the gully, and saturate the monster with daggers as it slowly backs up to where Lucia is. Repeat this strategy of leading it back and forth across the length of the chasm until its vitality bar gives out.

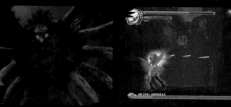

MISSION COMPLETE!	
S RANK REQUIREMENTS	
CLEAR TIME	4:00 MINUTES
ORBS	800
STYLISH AVERAGE	8 "SHOW TIME!!" COMBOS
DAMAGE	0
ITEM USED	NONE

REDEMPTION

Lucia has defeated her personal demons, as well as those who tried to force her destiny upon her. However, her story isn't over yet. With the opening of new game play modes and extra games, there are plenty of reasons to revisit Lucia's adventures.

SECRETS
SECRET ROOMS

Hidden throughout the missions on both discs are Secret Rooms where the demons wait to challenge the devil slayers in arena-style death matches. If you can defeat all the enemies, the exit will appear along with a Green Orb, a White Orb, and possibly a Blue Orb Fragment to help extend the character's vitality meter.

Secret Rooms are found by searching areas of note in the environment. Move to doors, windows, sewer gratings and even certain wall panels, and search to find a Secret Room. The first one you find will be Level 1, the next will be Level 2, and so on regardless of the order in which you find the locations during the missions. It doesn't matter if you find the locations in the right order, nor even in the same difficulty mode. All of the Secret Room locations are divulged as they occur in each mission of the chapters titled **Path 1: The Hunter** and **Path 2: The Protector**.

When you've found all the Secret Room locations in Normal Mode, you won't be able to find them again. However, when you play Hard Mode, they can all be found again. The same is true for Must Die Mode.

> ### FILL 'ER UP
> During harder missions, it's critical to find the secret rooms. Not only will you get some bonus Red Orbs, but you'll receive full Health and Devil Trigger gauges in the process.

DANTE'S SECRET ROOMS

All of Dante's even-numbered Secret Rooms, levels 1 through 20, will reward you with a Blue Orb Fragment when the enemies are defeated. In other words, you'll find them in Levels 2, 4, 6, 8, 10, etc. You can continue finding and conquering Secret Rooms after Level 20, but no longer will you receive Blue Orb Fragments.

LEVEL	ENEMY SET
1	AGONOFINIS
2	MSIRA
3	BRONTOMANCER, PYROMANCER
4	GOATLING
5	PUIA, GOATLING
6	HOMROMSIRA, GBUSMSIRA
7	INFESTANT
8	SPICERE, GOATLING
9	GBUSMSIRA
10	AUROMANCER, GOATLING
11	MORTFINIS
12	AUROMANCER, BRONTOMANCER
13	JOMOTHUMSIRA
14	ABYSS GOAT
15	SAVAGE GOLEM, GOATLING
16	FREKI & GERI
17	GOATLING
18	GOATLING, BLOOD GOAT
19	AUROMANCER, BLOOD GOAT
20	JOMOTHUMSIRA, HOMROMSIRA, ARIUS

LUCIA'S SECRET ROOMS

All of Lucia's Secret Rooms, levels 1 through 10, will reward you with a Blue Orb Fragment. While this means that her vitality gauge will increase more rapidly, there are fewer locations in the missions where Secret Rooms can be entered. As a result, if you miss one, you'll have to go back for it or play a harder difficulty mode!

LEVEL	ENEMY SET
1	PUIA
2	TERREOFINIS
3	PYROMANCER, AUROMANCER
4	SAVAGE GOLEM
5	AGONOFINIS (DISC TYPES), GOATLING
6	FLAMBAT
7	DEMONOCHORUS
8	SARGASSO
9	BLOOD GOAT
10	FREKI & GERI, BOLVERK

BONUSES AND SECRET CHARACTERS

Surmounting the impossible odds presented to the hunter and the protector in *Devil May Cry 2* awards the champion with extra modes of gameplay, new looks for the characters and secret characters!

BONUS MODES

Mission Select: Clear either character's game, and you'll be able to restart Normal Mode from any mission. This is helpful if you missed any Blue Orb Fragments or Secret Rooms. As you clear missions in Hard Mode and Must Die Mode, you'll be able to replay those chapters through the **Mission Select** screen.

Hard Mode: Clear Dante's disc and Lucia's disc to open Hard Mode. All Bonus Red Orb and Secret Room locations are reset, so that you can find them all again. Enemies have more vitality, and will use powerful new attacks not previously seen in Normal Mode.

Must Die Mode: Clear Hard Mode with Dante and Lucia to open "Dante Must Die!" and "Lucia Must Die!" Modes. All Bonus Red Orb and Secret Room locations are reset, so they can all be found again. Enemies have their maximum vitality, and will use rolling or spinning attacks that cannot be blocked. Additionally, after an enemy is onscreen for a short period of time they will enter their own version of Devil Trigger. An enemy that is luminescent blue or smoking with black energy is invulnerable to gunfire or projectiles. They cannot be knocked down or stunned, even by Devil Trigger attacks. The boss monsters will also Devil Trigger after a certain amount of time, which means they can only be damaged when the character is also in Devil Trigger and equipped with a certain Amulet Stone. Bon voyage!

The Bloody Palace

Complete Dante's and Lucia's missions on Normal Mode to unlock the Bloody Palace. This is a fantastic and challenging way to obtain all the Red Orbs you desire. The Bloody Palace takes place in more than 9,999 levels of sheer mayhem. To begin, load your

clear game save for either character and select "BLOODY PALACE" on the Mission Select screen. Extra costumes and bonus characters can be used in Bloody Palace.

Entering each room, you must defeat a set of enemies. The difficulty of the initial levels is dependent upon which difficulty modes you've cleared. In other words, if you've only finished Normal Mode, then Level 1 will contain one enemy. But if you're starting Bloody Palace after completing Must Die mode, then you'll face a continuous onslaught of foes.

When the room is cleared, three portals appear. The single-ring portal on the side transports you to the next level. The middle portal allows you to skip ten levels. The green-tinted portal on the other side allows you to skip a hundred levels. Since the difficulty increases with each new level, only you can best gauge how far ahead you should skip. If you go too far, you may find it impossible to continue.

The Bloody Palace ends only when your character dies. You'll be ranked according to the level reached, the time recorded, the number of enemies slain and the number of orbs collected. An amount of bonus orbs will be awarded as well, and you may save your game. The orbs you collect during Bloody Palace can be used during a mission to buy items or enhance weapons.

RESULT x999999
LEVEL   10000
TIME   1:11:39
ENEMY   2056
ORBS   45850
BONUS   99990

Each 10 levels, you'll fight a boss (at level 10, 20, 30, etc.). Not only is this a good way to expand the number of enemies in each character's Enemy file, but if you're strong enough to brave the hordes of enemies who often Devil Trigger, then eventually you'll reach level 9999. At that point, you will reenter the level over and over and fight all the bosses of the game. They can be damaged only while the character is in Devil Trigger, and only when equipped with a certain Amulets Stone. Good luck!

SECRET CHARACTERS & COSTUMES

New costumes and secret characters can be unlocked by defeating each game mode on both discs. Press L1 or R1 to switch costumes or characters while choosing a save game to load. Extra costumes and characters can also be used in Bloody Palace Mode.

Fashion Dante: Defeat Dante's missions on Normal Mode to unlock a stylish modern garb.

Fashion Lucia 1: Defeat Lucia's missions on Normal Mode to unlock her first fashionable costume, a rugged outdoor look.

Fashion

Lucia 2: Defeat Lucia's missions on Hard Mode to unlock a second more casual summer outfit.

Devil May Cry Dante with Force Edge: Defeat all of Dante's missions on Dante Must Die Mode to unlock his costume from the first game. The Rebellion sword will be replaced with a Max level Force Edge, Dante's original blade. Also, the combat music for all of Dante's missions is changed to the combat music from the first game.

Secretary: Defeat Lucia's missions on Lucia Must Die Mode to become able to replay the game as one of Arius' sexy bodyguards. In Devil Trigger, the Secretary looks more like a dark purple bird of prey

Trish

Defeat Dante's missions on Hard Mode to unlock Trish, the female heroine from the first *Devil May Cry*. Trish comes equipped with Dante's Handguns from the first game, as well as the Sword of Sparda. Complete Must Die Mode on Lucia's and Dante's discs, and Trish will also inherit the Nightmare. Trish also performs all of Dante's attack moves from the first game. The blonde bombshell can be played on both Dante's disc and Lucia's disc!

Trish's Moves

Shooting: Hold ☐ to fire normally. Tap ☐ rapidly to fire as frequently as the Submachine Guns! Trish fires normally or rapid fire from mid air as well.

Nightmare-Y: During underwater missions on Lucia's Disc, Trish automatically equips an upgraded version of the Nightmare-Beta weapon from the first Devil May Cry. This fires a beam that cuts through an enemy and ricochets off the nearest wall, then targets the next-closest foe. When used in Devil Trigger, Nightmare-Y shoot four beams at once!

Twosome Time: While locked onto a target (with or without holding R1), press the left analog stick toward an enemy close behind or to the side, and press ☐. Trish will target both enemies at once. The secondary foe will be knocked away, so this is a great defensive move to prevent being surrounded.

Flip Escape: Hold the Left Analog Stick in any direction and press the ◯ button to evade attacks.

Classic Air Hike: Press ✕ to jump, and press ✕ again while midair to jump even higher. The old magic circle still appears under Trish's feet, just like in the first game!

Kick Jump: Jump toward a wall, hold the Left Analog Stick toward the wall, and press ✕.

Wall Hike: Facing a wall, hold the Left Analog Stick toward the wall and press ◯. Trish runs up the wall and back-flips.

Wall Run: Running beside a wall, press ◯. Trish will run a short distance along the wall, and then side-flip off of the surface.

Sword Combo: Unlike Dante and Lucia, Trish performs one three-slash sword combo by pressing △ repeatedly. Holding the Left Analog Stick in a direction cannot modify this move.

High Time: Lock on to an enemy by holding R1 then hold the Left Analog Stick away from the foe and press △. Trish will bash the enemy into the sky. By pressing △ hard during the move, Trish will leap up into the air with the enemy. Press △ again while in the air with the enemy to knock them out of the sky to the ground.

Stinger: Lock on to an enemy by holding R1 , press the Left Analog Stick in the direction of the targeted enemy and press △. Trish shoots across the ground and pierces the enemy with a hard stab. This move knocks most enemies to the ground.

Sashimi: Perform the first two slashes of Trish's Sword Combo. As she swings back with the second stroke, begin tapping △ rapidly. Trish rapidly spears an enemy multiple times, and then flings them away with a short Stinger attack.

Classic Round Trip: After the first sword slash, hold △ until Trish sheathes the sword. When you release △, Trish flings Sparda at the closest target. The sword spins around the foe, slashing it and any other nearby foes repeatedly. The sword will continue spinning in place for five seconds, allowing you to shoot other enemies or perform all of the classic Ifrit moves.

Punch and Kick Combo: Perform Classic Round Trip, then press △ while the sword is spinning. Trish attacks enemies with two punches and two roundhouse kicks.

Ifrit Kick13: Perform Classic Round Trip, then hold R1 to lock on, press the Left Analog Stick *toward* the target, and press △ while the sword is spinning. Trish flies at enemies and kicks them roundhouse style with a fiery foot!

Ifrit Magma Drive: Perform Classic Round Trip, hold R1 to lock on, press the Left Analog Stick *away* from the target, and press △ while the sword is spinning. Trish delivers a powerful flaming uppercut to a foe, knocking them into the sky!

Ifrit Air Kick: Perform Classic Round Trip, then jump or Air Hike into the sky. Press △ at the height of the jump, and Trish launches herself at the closest enemy to deliver a fiery kick that stuns the monster.

Devil Trigger: Press L1 when the Devil Trigger gauges are full. Trish dons sunglasses and glows with her unearthly power. While in this state, Trish moves faster and can use the powers of the various Amulet Stones.

Classic Air Raid: Equip the Aerial Heart and Devil Trigger. Press the ✕ button to fly high in the air, and press ☐ to attack with massive beams of demonic energy. This attack decimates even the long vitality bars of boss monsters in no time! Unlike the other Air Raid attacks, this one is styled after the same move in the previous game.

Devil Trigger Round Trip: Equip the Aerial Heart and Devil Trigger. While flying in the sky, press △. Similar to Dante's same move, Trish flings her sword in a short arc, and it spins through all the targets at close range.

Super Morph

Whenever Dante's health falls into the red, he can transform into the ultimate Devil Trigger form if his power meter is filled to at least the first gauge. Leaping high into the air, the Super Morph form can fly even without the Aerial Heart equipped. The giant demon form has only two attacks: ☐ button causes the Super Morph to launch fireballs with both hands. Press △ button repeatedly to perform a sword combo with two beam blades that extend from the monster's gauntlets. Dante is invincible while in Super Morph form, and cannot be hurt even by boss monsters. However, once Super Morph is triggered, you cannot exit this state until all the power has run out of the Devil Trigger gauges.

OFFICIAL STRATEGY GUIDE

BY DAN BIRLEW

Brady Publishing

An Imprint of Pearson Education

201 West 103rd Street

Indianapolis, Indiana 46290

ISBN: 0-7440-0227-3

Library of Congress Catalog No.: 2002116965

Printing Code: The rightmost double-digit number is the year of the book's printing; the rightmost single-digit number is the number of the book's printing. For example, 02-1 shows that the first printing of the book occurred in 2002.

06 05 04 03   4 3 2 1

Manufactured in the United States of America.

ACKNOWLEDGEMENTS

The author wishes to acknowledge the contributions of the many individuals who help to make this guide a success. Thanks to Robb Kneebone and the Argosy Publishing staff, for their top-notch work on the maps and their professionalism. Thanks to Leigh Davis, for letting me do this project after I whined and begged for it. Thanks to David Waybright, for his valiant last minute efforts to get me that new build on Christmas Eve. Thanks to Michael Owen, for all his great work on the screenshots in all of BradyGames' books, and for checking my walkthrough on this one. Thanks to Christian Sumner, for letting me pull my hair out over the telephone and being a decisive project leader. Thanks to Aunt Patti for the toolbox. Finally special thanks to my wife Laura for being my gymnastics terminology consultant (using her championship cheerleading expertise for good instead of evil).

ABOUT THE AUTHOR

Dan Birlew lives in southern Nevada with his wife Laura and the Freunds. He is the author of twenty one titles published by BradyGames, including official strategy guides for titles such as *Resident Evil Zero*, *Onimusha 2: Samurai's Destiny*, *Resident Evil* and *Devil May Cry*. If he ever gets a chance to take a breath, he hopes to build a workbench in his garage.

BRADYGAMES ACKNOWLEDGEMENTS

BradyGames would like to thank everyone at Argosy Publishing for getting the maps to us in an insanely short amount of time.

BRADYGAMES STAFF

Publisher
David Waybright

Editor-In-Chief
H. Leigh Davis

Creative Director
Robin Lasek

Marketing Manager
Janet Eshenour

Licensing Manager
Mike Degler

Assistant Marketing Manager
Susie Nieman

CREDITS

Project Editor
Christian Sumner

Screenshot Editor
Michael Owen

Book Designer
Doug Wilkins

Cover and Poster Designer
Carol Stamile

Production Designer
Tracy Wehmeyer

Maps
Argosy Publishing